Deer Hunting

Deer Hunting

RICHARD P. SMITH

STACKPOLE BOOKS

DEER HUNTING
Copyright © 1978 by
Richard P. Smith

Published by
STACKPOLE BOOKS
Cameron and Kelker Streets
P.O. Box 1831
Harrisburg, Pa. 17105

Published simultaneously in Don Mills, Ontario, Canada by Thomas Nelson &
Sons, Ltd.

Printed in the U.S.A.

Library of Congress Cataloging in Publication Data

Smith, Richard P., 1949–
  Deer hunting.

  Bibliography: p.
  Includes index.
  1. Deer hunting—North America.   I. Title.
SK301.S66   799.2'77'357   78-4660
ISBN 0-8117-0493-9

To my father,
who taught me to be
a sportsman

Contents

Acknowledgments

I would like to take this opportunity to thank all of my friends and relatives who have let me be a part of their deer hunts. Every experience made me a better and richer hunter.

My dad deserves recognition, of course, for cultivating my interest in hunting. George Smith, an uncle, deserves special appreciation for making many of my deer hunts possible. Leonard Yelle, another uncle, took me on my first successful deer hunt. My brother Bruce has shared many deer hunts with me. Rudy Rudibaugh taught me about mule deer and how to hunt them.

Beryl Jensen, Ed Lindstrom, Mike Hogan, Fred and Tom DeRocher, Jim Haveman, Dave Raikko, Bob DeLongchamp, Bill Robinson, Phil Doepke, Kirwin Werner, Keith Chapel, and many more can be added to the list.

This book wouldn't have been possible without the help of Ken Lowe who gave me the encouragement necessary to start writing and Dave Richey who has assisted in countless ways. My friends and relatives have all been a source of encouragement in this endeavor, especially my wife Lucy.

Last, but not least, the state and provincial Departments of Fish and Game and Natural Resources deserve thanks for providing information that went into this book.

Introduction

I was all set to write a lengthy introduction, but remembering the speaker at the podium who didn't want to bore his audience, I won't. This book is about deer and deer hunting; it's as simple as that. The table of contents tells you exactly what is included. If you have any interest in whitetails or mule deer there is something in this book for you.

Researching and writing this book has made me a more knowledgeable deer hunter. If you learn as much from reading these words as I have from writing them, both efforts will have been worthwhile.

1

About the Quarry

There are two native species of deer in North America: the whitetail and mule deer. Within each species a number of subspecies exists that exhibit variations that set them apart from each other. Some of the variations are minor, others are more noticeable.

A total of 30 subspecies of whitetails have been identified in North America. Seventeen of these are found in the United States and Canada (48 contiguous states and eight provinces). Another 13 exist south of the border. Where subspecies overlap, they frequently interbreed. Some states have more than one race of whitetails.

The northern whitetail is the largest and most widely spread of the subspecies. A 425-pound (live' weight) member of this variety is the heaviest known specimen. It was shot in Michigan. Northern whitetails are found in 17 states and five Canadian provinces. They include Michigan, Minnesota, Wisconsin, New York, New Jersey, Massachusetts, New Hampshire, Maryland, Pennsylvania, Ohio, Delaware, Indiana, Illinois, Connecticut, Rhode Island, Maine, Vermont, Ontario, Quebec, Manitoba, New Brunswick, and Nova Scotia.

Virginia whitetails are found in Virginia, the Carolinas, Kentucky, Georgia, Mississippi, Tennessee, and Alabama.

Dakota whitetails inhabit the Dakotas, Kansas, Wyoming, Nebraska, Montana, Manitoba, Saskatchewan, and Alberta.

The northwest variety calls the states of Oregon, Idaho, Montana, Washington, Nevada, California, and Utah home. They also reside in British Columbia and Alberta in Canada.

In contrast to most other whitetails, the Columbian subspecies is endangered. They are only found in Oregon and Washington.

Coues, or fantail, whitetails inhabit desert regions of California, Arizona, New Mexico, and Mexico.

The Texas whitetail is also found in parts of New Mexico and Mexico as well as in Texas, Kansas, Colorado, and Oklahoma.

A Kansas strain lives in its home state plus Oklahoma, Nebraska, Arkansas, eastern Texas, Missouri, Iowa, and Louisiana.

Florida coastal whitetails are distributed in Florida's panhandle, southern Alabama, and Mississippi.

Eight subspecies of whitetails in the U.S. have very limited distribution as indicated by their names: Carmen Mountains (Texas); Avery Island (Texas and Louisiana); Bull's Island, Hunting Island, and Hilton Head Island (all in South Carolina); Blackbeard Island (Georgia); Florida (Georgia and Florida); and the Florida Keys whitetail, the smallest of the species. Keys deer, like the Columbian type, are protected.

Some species of whitetails have been introduced into areas where they wouldn't otherwise be found, which may account for some variations in the distributions listed above.

There are 11 subspecies of mule deer, but they are commonly lumped into four categories. The Rocky Mountain variety is the most widely distributed. Desert mule deer, Columbian blacktails, and sitka blacktails are the other three types.

Mule deer are primarily western animals. They are found from the southeastern portion of Alaska to northern Mexico. Their extreme eastern limit includes western portions of Iowa, Minnesota, Kansas, Oklahoma, and Texas. They live all along the Pacific Coast as far as and including the Baja Peninsula. In Canada representatives of the species have invaded the southern limits of the Yukon and Northwest Territories. They are common in British Columbia, Alberta, Saskatchewan, and the southwest corner of Manitoba.

As with some of the subspecies of whitetails, mule deer are not hunted in every state or province where they are found. Low densities in the extreme limits of their range are not huntable populations.

Columbian blacktails call Washington, Oregon, California, and British Columbia home. Sitkas occupy the northern portion of the mule deer range in Alaska, the Yukon, and British Columbia. Desert and Rocky Mountain muleys occupy the rest of this deer's range.

The variety of subspecies of whitetail and mule deer basically reflect variations in size, coat color, tail markings, and other habitat adaptations. Most whitetails look alike. To the untrained observer, it can be

Mule deer have small, black-tipped tails with white rumps. The tines fork on bucks as shown by this fine specimen *(photo credit: Bob Landis)*.

difficult to tell many of the subspecies from the others. The differences among the blacktail subspecies and mule deer are more apparent.

Muleys have narrow, ropelike tails. The undersides of mule deer tails are hairless. When running, this deer holds its tail clamped against its distinctive white rump. Blacktail tails are wider than those of mule deer. Whitetails have longer, wider tails than all types of mule deer. Their tails are brown on the back with white trim. The species gets its name from the white underside, which is visible when the deer waves his tail from side to side in an elevated position while he runs.

There is also an obvious difference between the structure of antlers worn by adult whitetails and those carried by mature mule deer bucks. Typical whitetail racks exhibit unbranched tines arising from main beams. Points beyond the brow tine on mule deer antlers typically fork. Blacktail antlers are generally smaller than those of their mule deer relatives.

Another feature that usually varies between mule and whitetail deer is ear size. Muleys typically have larger ears than whitetails. Coues whitetails have larger ears than normal for the species, which is thought to be an adaptation for their desert environment.

A less obvious external difference between whitetail and mule deer is the size of their metatarsal glands. Metatarsals are located on the outside of the lower hind legs of deer. A patch of white hair marks the location of each metatarsal. Metatarsals are about an inch long on whitetails, over two inches on blacktails, and about five inches on other mule deer.

Whitetails and muleys have three additional external glands. Tarsal glands are on the inside of the hind legs at the joint. Interdigital glands are found between the toes on each foot. Preorbitals are directly in the corner of the eyes; these release tears to cleanse their eyes.

When running, the two species can be differentiated by their gait. Mule deer employ a stiff-legged bounce. Whitetails run in typical head-long fashion, but also make lengthy leaps or bounds. Deer may cover as much as 30 feet in a forward leap or bound. Whitetails have scaled barriers eight and one-half feet high.

Top speed for mule deer has been clocked at from 25 to 30 miles an hour. Whitetails are capable of speeds from 35 to 40 miles per hour, but are probably moving at closer to 20 or 25 miles per hour under hunting conditions.

Most deer hunters overestimate the average size, both in height and weight, of deer. Mule deer will measure from 36 to 42 inches high at the shoulder. The smaller blacktails stand a maximum of 38 inches at the shoulder. Big whitetail bucks will measure 36 inches at the shoulder. The smallest whitetails (Keys deer) stand only 24 to 26 inches high.

Estimated live weight of the biggest mule deer is 475 pounds. Average field-dressed weights for adult bucks fall in a range from 150 to 200 pounds. Northern whitetails are about the same. Dressed

Most hunters overestimate the height of deer. This whitetail being used for a browse selection study isn't even waist high on researcher Bill Bauer. It would take a big buck to measure 36 inches at the shoulder.

This young whitetail only weighs 80 pounds. The average weight of muleys and whitetails (adults) is about 150 pounds. The largest representative of each species has been over 400 pounds.

weights of blacktails and southern whitetails range from 80 to 150 pounds.

Generally, deer will lose one-fifth of their weight during field dressing. A rough determination of a whitetail's or muley's live weight can be made by dividing the dressed weight by four, then adding the resulting number to the dressed weight. The weights listed below (dressed weight first, followed by live weight) should be accurate in most cases: 80, 105; 90, 115; 100, 130; 110, 140; 120, 155; 130, 165; 140, 180; 150, 190; 160, 205; 170, 215; 180, 230; 190, 240; 200, 255.

Bucks may lose as much as 20 percent of their weight during the breeding season (rut), which occurs in the fall.

15

Deer are color blind. They see shades of black and white. Movement attracts their attention. Hunters who remain motionless are often a source of curiosity rather than alarm. The whitetail and mule deers' sight is better to the sides than straight ahead because of the position of their eyes. Animals that live in open country tend to depend on their vision more than those in heavily wooded terrain.

It isn't unusual to have deer cautiously approach an immobile person they can't smell. They recognize the object as an addition to the landscape, but are unsure of what it is, so are curious. Sometimes they nervously stamp a front foot if they suspect danger. I have frequently seen deer do this while I was bowhunting or trying to photograph them. Occasionally, a wise doe will whirl as if to run off, but then will stop quickly and look back in an apparent attempt to catch me in the act of moving.

The sense of hearing is well developed in deer. Only sounds that are not normal in their environment, such as human voices, metallic sounds, fabric rubbing against brush, or noisy human feet, unduly alarm them.

Deer rely heavily on their sense of smell. It is probably their strongest defense against hunters. If the wind is right, deer often smell intruders before they are within sight of their quarry. Animals that "wind" hunters sometimes make a noise by blowing through their nostrils. This sound is often referred to as a snort. Both bucks and does make this sound. It serves as a warning signal to other deer in the area. The noise they make sounds like a train whistle or someone blowing on an empty rifle cartridge.

Whitetails and muleys don't often make sounds with their mouths, but they do occasionally. The most common vocalizations are between does and fawns when the offspring are young, between bucks and does during the rut, and from deer that are distressed. These sounds are seldom heard by hunters though. On two occasions while hunting I have heard bucks following does during the rut make noises. They were very distinctive, throaty, rasping sounds. The exact sounds are hard to describe. I have heard penned bucks make similar noises. While deer are being handled by biologists during live trapping and marking operations, they sometimes bleat or baa.

Both whitetails and the blacktail variety of mule deer inhabit thick, brushy terrain. Blacktail habitat rivals whitetail country for denseness and short-sight distances in many cases. The larger varieties of mule deer are usually found in more open terrain than either black or whitetails, but they can be found in stands of timber, too.

Mule deer are generally considered a migratory species of deer;

whitetails usually spend their entire lives in a limited home range of two square miles, and in many cases, less. The truth of the matter is that both species exhibit these traits.

Most mule deer have distinct summer and winter ranges. Summers are often spent at higher elevations than winters. There is a downhill migration in the fall to escape heavy snows. As the snow melts in the spring or early summer the deer move uphill. Whitetails that live in mountainous or hilly terrain do the same thing. In South Dakota's Black Hills, for example, whitetails migrate between their low winter range and high summer range twice a year. Distance of travel is as great as 20 miles.

Some whitetail deer in northern climates migrate to wintering areas called yards, which are primarily lowland swampy areas. Deer yards vary in size from a few square miles to hundreds of square miles. To reach yarding areas, many deer move south, toward an area where snow depths are less. Most of the time there is little or no elevation change between yards and summer range.

Deer that make seasonal movements, regardless of species, often use the same routes year after year, unless habitat change requires an adjustment.

Most whitetail deer spend their lives in a limited home range. Some blacktails and mule deer have adapted similarly where the climate permits it. Whitetails mark and defend a territory during the breeding season. Mule deer are generally not territorial, roaming at will during the summer as well as the fall. Muleys spooked by hunters may travel miles to a new area. Whitetails seldom roam far. If pushed out of their territory, they usually return.

In the wild most bucks don't live past three or four years, but older ones occur in remote or lightly hunted terrain. Does tend to live longer than bucks because they aren't as sought after by hunters. The oldest whitetails and mule deer occur in captivity where ages of 19 and 22 years have been recorded. Ten-year-old deer are not common in the wild.

The most common method of determining the age of deer is by examining their cheek teeth. Fawns generally have four cheek teeth on each of the upper and lower jaws. Three are premolars and one is a molar. Yearlings exhibit two more molars, although one is usually not showing completely. By age two and one-half all molars are completely visible and the three premolars, which were temporary, have been replaced by permanent premolars. After that point the amount of tooth wear is an indicator of age. Criteria for determining age by tooth wear vary slightly between species of deer and even the same species found in different regions.

A buck's age is seldom reflected by the number of tines on his antlers. Beam circumference of antlers is more closely related to age. In Nebraska, for instance, if the beam circumference one inch above the burr is greater than 3 5/16 inches on whitetails, the buck is usually two and one-half years or older. Mule deer of the same age will have a circumference greater than 3 1/16 inches.

Bucks are polygamous. When mature they service a number of does. Bucks are capable of impregnating about 20 does, but this is seldom necessary in the wild unless there is an extremely lopsided sex ratio. The rut usually takes place from October to December, but may be as late as February and March in some parts of the south.

Under optimum conditions a percentage of young-of-the-year does will produce fawns. In poor habitat does may not be productive until they are two and one-half years old. Does must breed within a 24-hour period when in heat. If they don't, they will come into breeding condition again at 28-day intervals. Most adult does give birth to one or two fawns, but triplets are possible. The gestation period for deer is seven months.

At birth fawns usually weigh from five to eight pounds. The

Fawns weigh from five to eight pounds at birth. This one is attempting to walk on wobbly legs.

18

Fawns lose their spotted coats three or four months after birth. The mottled coloring serves to camouflage young deer.

percentage of bucks born is normally slightly higher than does. Young deer rely on their spotted coat to camouflage them against predators. If fawns are scentless at birth, the condition lasts for a short time. When one to three weeks old, deer are able to run well. Milk is the primary source of nourishment for deer during their first two or three months of life, but they begin foraging on grass between two and three weeks old. When a month old, fawns often eat solid foods. They are usually weaned by three months of age, but may continue nursing after that time.

Fawns lose their spotted coats between three and four months old. Adults go through two coat changes a year. A reddish-colored summer coat replaces the winter pelage in late spring or early summer. The heavier, darker winter dress takes its place in the fall.

The piebald (partially white) deer represents the most common coat color mutation.

Abnormalities in coat color are exhibited by some deer. Partial albinos (piebald deer) are most common. These mutants exhibit varying degrees of white, but don't have the pink eyes of true albinos. Melanistic deer (black-colored) are not as common as albinos; in fact, they are very rare.

I once had the opportunity to photograph a true albino whitetail doe. She was a strange sight. Her eyes, ears, and nose were pink; and she was all white except for the tarsal glands on the back legs. There were plenty of normal deer in the area that seemed to accept her presence. She was spookier than the other animals though.

Additional abnormalities occur with varying frequencies in deer herds. Does with antlers are not uncommon. Some have small antlers in velvet. Antler growth is caused by abnormal amounts of male hormones. Nonetheless, these does breed normally. Does with polished antlers are usually hermaphroditic, that is, they have both male and female sex organs and are often sterile.

Occasionally, bucks will grow three antlers. There is a record of a Canadian buck that sprouted a third antler on its nose. A Montana buck developed an extra antler below its right eye. Castrated bucks or those with hormonal imbalance may grow oddball antlers, fail to shed their velvet, or not develop antlers at all.

Short lower jaws show on some deer. This mutation doesn't affect a

True albinos, like this doe with pink eyes, nose, and inside of the ears, are rare.

My brother Bruce shot this short-jawed doe. The deformity didn't affect its health.

deer's ability to feed. My brother shot a short-jawed doe that was eight or ten years old and in good health.

Warts or tumors called papillomas or fibromas are found on deer, too. In bad cases they give the animals an unappealing appearance. These tumors are usually not malignant nor do they affect the edibility of venison from a whitetail or mule deer that has them. Warts are commonly on the head, but they may occur elsewhere on the body.

With one exception, disease doesn't affect deer to a significant extent. A viral disease, which is thought to be transmitted by an insect carrier, called Epizootic Hemorrhagic Disease (EHD) accounts for significant losses in various parts of the U.S. Ninety percent of the deer exposed to the virus usually die.

Diseased animals develop a fever, lose their appetite, and have difficulty breathing. The fever seems to induce excessive thirst so deer that succumb to EHD are often found near water. Before death, deer go into a state of shock. The disease causes destruction of blood vessel walls causing hemorrhaging. EHD outbreaks occur in the summer. Incidence of the disease ceases after a frost.

There was a recorded outbreak of hoof-and-mouth disease among mule deer in California during 1924. Since that time, its occurrence has been minimal.

Additional deer losses are related to parasite infestations. Significant mortality has occurred among Alabama's herd, for one, as a result of lungworm. Other internal parasites that sometimes cause problems are brainworm, liver flukes, and nasal botfly larvae. External parasites include lice and ticks.

Parasites, both internal and external, are common in and on deer, but their incidence is low in healthy whitetail and mule deer herds. Problems from parasites normally arise in populations on poor range or when herds overpopulate an area.

Extremes in weather such as prolonged cold winters, floods, and hurricanes take further tolls on deer. Here again, healthy deer herds are least susceptible to these conditions. Thousands of whitetails and muleys also die on highways yearly as a result of collisions with automobiles. Less significant accidents account for more deer deaths, including getting stuck in fences and trees and falls.

Predation is probably the most common mortality factor among deer herds. Mountain lions, wolves, bobcats and coyotes all take their toll, but man is the most important predator of deer today. Planned predation through hunting is the best means of maintaining healthy deer populations. The reproductive capacity of whitetail and mule deer is geared toward annual production of surplus animals in response to the

Countless deer are hit by cars every year.

many mortality factors they are subject to. If the surplus isn't removed through predation, population compensation will occur through disease, extremes in weather, road kills, and other accidents.

Losses to disease, weather, and accidents are less desirable than predation as a means of controlling deer populations. Adequate annual harvest through hunting will keep deer mortality from other causes at a minimum. For more information on deer management, refer to chapter 17.

Fawns normally stay with their mothers through the winter and into the next spring. Does chase their offspring from the previous year away before giving birth to more fawns. Disowned yearlings sometimes travel long distances before settling into a home range of their own. Most, however, probably disperse less than five miles from the area where they were raised.

Nebraska and South Dakota have some interesting findings on dispersal of young whitetail and mule deer. In South Dakota ten male mule deer tagged as fawns moved an average of 36.7 miles from that time to when they were killed as yearlings or adults. Some whitetails also disperse over long distances. Twenty-tree members of this species showed an average movement of 38 miles in Nebraska. A pair of whitetails traveled 125 and 137 miles from points where they were tagged to points of recovery in that state.

Bucks frequently seek the company of others of their sex before the

Predation is the most commonly accepted mortality factor of deer, and man is the most important predator.

rut starts. From my experiences mule deer males seem to be more gregarious than whitetails. Once breeding begins the same group of bucks may fight among one another in competition for does. In these contests the stronger of the two deer usually wins out without any injury to either contestant. Occasionally, however, the animals antlers will become hopelessly locked. Both deer usually die.

Broken antlers and superficial injuries sometimes result from fights

Marking young deer with a collar is a good way to determine how far they disperse, if at all, by the time they mature. Average dispersal for muleys in South Dakota and whitetails in Nebraska was 36.7 and 38 miles respectively.

In the summer, groups of bucks can be seen together and are congenial, but once the rut starts they sometimes fight *(photo credit: Bob Landis)*.

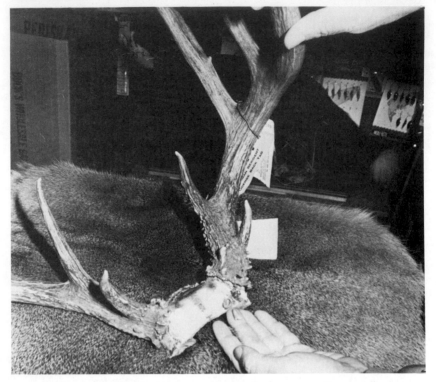

This broken tine was removed from the skull of a whitetail buck. He probably broke it in a fight.

between bucks, too. Last fall, a local taxidermist found a broken tine imbedded in the skull of a buck's head he was skinning. Apparently, the piece of antler was lost by another buck in a fight.

Whitetail and mule deer are good swimmers. Reports of them swimming for miles are common. When chased by dogs or predators, deer sometimes head for water to escape them. Animals may also go in water to escape insect bites during the summer. Some deer feed on aquatic vegetation in the summer, too.

Basically, whitetail and mule deer are browsers, but they also graze on grasses and weeds when they are available. Additionally, deer are fond of a variety of agricultural crops. Leaves from trees and plants make up a large part of their diet in the summer and some in the fall. They do most of their browsing in late fall and winter. Woody material such as the buds and the tender tips of saplings and shrubs from sagebrush, mountain mahogany, dogwood, willow, maple, and oak are preferred. Evergreen leaves from yew, cedar, juniper, hemlock, and some pines are also favored. Acorns, beech nuts, and apples are prime fall and winter deer foods when available. It is not uncommon for deer to stand on their hind legs to reach morsels of food on trees, especially in the winter when rations are sometimes in short supply.

Deer break or pull woody material that they ingest. Since they only have teeth on the lower jaw in front, they can't bite through stems. For this reason, the ends of limbs or stems that deer feed on will be ragged. Further back in the mouth, deer have teeth on both the top and bottom jaws, which are used for chewing.

Ingested food is chewed when taken in, but is later chewed again. Deer have four cavities in their stomachs: the rumen, reticulum, omasum and abomasum. When first swallowed, food goes in the rumen. Bacteria are mixed with the material here to help break it down. The strain of bacteria in the rumen depends on what type of food is being consumed; so bacteria may vary during different seasons of the year. Cuds of food are regurgitated from the rumen then rechewed.

Deer are primarily browsers. This one is munching on cedar.

The digestion process is completed in the other three cavities of the stomach.

Whitetails and mule deer require an average of five to ten pounds of food per 100 pounds of weight a day. Food requirements are greatest during periods of cold weather.

A fairly recent biological discovery about deer in areas where winters are typically severe is they go into a physiological state similar to hibernation during the height of the cold season. The animals don't go to sleep, but their metabolism slows down. It seems to be an adaptation for conserving energy reserves necessary to carry them through the critical period.

2

Where to Hunt

One of the first steps on the way to a satisfying deer hunt is to choose where to hunt wisely. To do so often takes time and effort, but every consideration this phase of the hunt gets can prove to be well worth it. The process of picking the best location possible increases anticipation of the upcoming season and adds an important touch of confidence to a trip, which can make the difference between success and failure.

Planning where to go on a deer hunt should be done as far in advance of the season as possible. Most of the work involved can be done from home. This stage of deer hunting fills the gap from one season to the next. It is homework deer hunters shouldn't mind doing.

Preseason selection of an area for deer season is important on any deer hunt, but it is vital in some states. These states require hunters to specify a region or management unit in which they wish to hunt. That area is marked on their licenses and restricts them to hunting within that locality. This requirement will probably become more prevalent in the future.

Planning where to go is just as important for deer hunters who hunt in their home region or state as it is for those who travel to another state. On the average, deer hunters who confine their hunting to home territory know little about deer densities a county or two away and so miss out on what might be better deer hunting. These fellows hunt the same locations year after year and often accept the hunting available in their spots as representative of what is available throughout the region or state. In many cases this is far from the truth.

My home region, the Upper Peninsula of Michigan, will serve as a perfect illustration of how deer densities can vary regionally. Some of the best and some of the worst deer hunting in the state can be found in this 15-county area. Northern counties that border on Lake Superior have mature forests and long, cold winters. Farming is common in southern counties of the region, younger forests are also found there, and winters aren't as severe as further north. Some of the best deer hunting in the state is found in southern counties. A drive of 50 to 100 miles from the north to the south in upper Michigan can take hunters from poor to excellent deer hunting.

Deer density is one of the most important considerations in deciding where to hunt, but other factors must be considered, too. These include hunter densities, availability of public land to hunt on, and antler growth. Many times where there are the most deer, there will also be the most hunters. I, for one, do not like to hunt deer in locations where the odds favor seeing more hunters than whitetails or mule deer. If little or no public land is available in an area of high deer density, permission must be obtained to hunt. When that isn't possible, an alternate locality must be sought. Deer hunters interested in trophy heads won't often find them in areas of high deer concentrations, unless the spot is lightly hunted.

When interested in hunting out of state, a number of additional factors should be considered. They include season dates, bag limits, availability of licenses, license fees, and hunter success ratios. Sometimes season dates and differing hunter success are considerations from area to area in one state, too.

Most of the necessary information on deer densities, harvest figures, hunter success, seasons, licenses, antler growth, and availability of public land can be obtained from state fish and game agencies or departments of natural resources. All states publish an annual hunting digest that contains pertinent information on licenses and seasons. Outdoor magazines are sources of information on seasons and license fees, too. *Outdoor Life,* for example, publishes state-by-state and province-by-province listings every fall. The National Rifle Association also publishes a hunting annual that is packed with helpful facts.

Most game departments also have lists of deer harvests, populations or indices that reflect their general abundance by county, management unit, districts, or regions. The highest harvests normally occur where deer numbers are highest. Hunt digests and harvest figures will often be available upon written request to the state agency's main office. The addresses of these are given in chapter 3. A regional or district office would be a better source of information if you are interested in only a portion of a state or province.

Maps that show public and private lands should also be available from state or provincial offices. Some times there is a charge for these. If maps aren't available from state offices, try other sources. In Michigan, for instance, the Michigan United Conservation Clubs publishes a booklet of county maps for the entire state. Platt books can be obtained from individual counties, and U.S. Forest Service offices normally have maps of any areas under their control.

Maps are not only good references for determining land ownership, but they can also be used to determine where roadless tracts of land are located. Areas without roads that are at least a square mile in size are prime locations for getting away from large numbers of deer hunters. Few hunters penetrate far into tracts that aren't easily accessible.

Wildlife biologists are usually the best contacts for queries on deer densities, antler growth, and hunter success. A phone call or personal visit is generally the best way to reach biologists for information. Try to write questions down on paper before calling or stopping in, to prevent forgetting what you want to ask.

The Boone and Crockett and Pope and Young record books are great references for learning where most of the big-antlered bucks are taken in individual states. The seventh edition of *North American Big Game*, which lists all record deer heads taken with firearms, was published recently in conjunction with the National Rifle Association. If you are looking for a record or trophy head, these books will give you an idea of what parts of a state or which states big racks come from. Additional large-racked bucks are likely to be found in regions where others were bagged. Characteristics of the habitat in these parts of the country plus the genetics of the herd are often conducive to producing outstanding antlers on bucks.

Virginia, Pennsylvania, Ohio, and some other states have big buck clubs. Their records show where trophy heads are likely to be found within their state.

When planning a deer hunt, try to dig up as much information as possible that will be helpful in determining which state and which region within it is most likely to provide the deer hunt you want.

To illustrate how to go about choosing a place to hunt deer, let's look at a couple of examples. For convenience sake we will assume our hunters want to hunt somewhere in the Upper Peninsula of Michigan. The first group of hunters want to see deer. They will be satisfied with any legal whitetail—other hunters in the area won't bother them.

Michigan's Department of Natural Resources (DNR) compiles a yearly list of the number of deer seen by its field personnel for each county. The number of hours involved in the sightings is also noted. This information is used to determine the average number of deer seen for every 100 hours DNR employees are in the field. The figures for each county represent an index of the general abundance of deer there. It is easy to determine which county has the highest density of deer by comparing the number of animals seen per 100 hours in each one.

Menominee County stands out as the number-one choice for our hunters. For 1976, July through August, an average of 165 deer were seen for every 100 hours in deer country. The next highest count was 52.5, which was for Dickinson County.

A check of the 1976 deer harvest by counties would show there were an average of more than two bucks per square mile taken by hunters in Menominee County, which is as high as the harvest gets in Michigan. Further checking would show there were from seven to 12 hunters per square mile in Menominee County during the '76 seasons, which is about medium pressure. Part of the reason for the lower-than-expected hunting pressure is private ownership of much of the county's land.

A look at a county map would show that since there is enough public land to choose from there wouldn't be any problem finding a place to hunt if permission couldn't be obtained to hunt on private property. Heavy hunting pressure isn't always the rule in areas with limited public hunting land and lots of deer. I have hunted for days at a time in locations in both Menominee and Dickinson counties (hunter density is

Look for places that are difficult to reach when hunting in areas with a lot of deer to avoid other hunters.

Hunting from horseback is a good way to get away from crowds of deer hunters.

supposed to be as high as 20 per square mile in Dickinson) without seeing any hunters who didn't belong to our group. Few hunters spend the effort to reach out-of-the-way locations. One area we frequent is surrounded by a marshy bog. We wear chest waders to get across the marsh, then put boots on when we reach dry ground.

Horses provide a convenient means of transportation to get away from crowds of hunters when hunting mule deer in Western states.

Another group of hunters are interested in trying for trophy bucks in upper Michigan. They would find that four bucks from upper Michigan qualified for Boone and Crockett listing by looking at the current edition of *North American Big Game*. Two of them were taken in Iron County and one each in Alger and Baraga counties. Iron County would be their best choice for big-racked bucks if that was their only concern.

If they wanted to compete with as few hunters as possible, Alger or Baraga county might be a better selection. Hunting pressure figures show there were seven to 12 hunters per square mile in Iron County for 1976. Alger County had 4.6 to 7 hunters per square mile, and Baraga had less than 4.5.

Knowledge of deer densities in these counties would make the choice between them fairly easy. An average of 22.3 deer were seen per 100 hours in Alger, but only 3.6 in Baraga. An average of 31.4 deer were seen for every 100 hours spent in Iron County.

Public hunting land wouldn't be a problem in any of those three big buck counties.

The same sort of information used in these examples can be used to help determine where best to hunt in any region, state, or province, providing it is available. When hunting out-of-state, such factors as the number of licenses available to nonresidents must also be considered. Some states sell their quotas, at least those for preferred areas, well in advance of season openings.

After general hunting locations have been determined hunters should concern themselves with isolating the best huntable-size chunks of terrain available. We have already seen that deer densities are not the same thoughout a state. By the same token their distribution is not equal throughout a square mile of cover. There can be 10 whitetails or muleys utilizing an area a fraction of that size and only a few throughout the rest of it. Some portions of deer habitat are simply more attractive to the animals than others.

Sources of large quantities of high-quality food are great for attracting concentrations of deer. Agricultural crops are favored by whitetail and mule deer. A good crop of acorns will attract a lot of local deer, too. Other favored haunts of deer are areas that have been burned or

Islands are often good places to hunt.

logged in recent years. Young vegetation that muleys and whitetails thrive on grows profusely in either type of opening.

When in hilly or mountainous terrain the biggest bucks are usually found at the highest elevations. Islands in lakes or large rivers also can be hotspots for deer hunting. Whitetails and muleys that reside on some islands aren't often disturbed. The same is true of any piece of deer habitat that is exceptionally thick or difficult to reach.

Some of these locations can be pinpointed on maps. Talking with wildlife biologists, conservation officers or game wardens, sport shop owners, and other deer hunters in the area you plan to hunt is a good idea, too. From that point on, the final decision of where to hunt should be made after spending time in the field.

There is one more consideration that can play a decisive role in determining where to hunt deer for some hunters. That factor is familiarity. Hunters who have spent a season or two or maybe a dozen in one area are bound to become familiar with the terrain, its deer, and the deer's behavior. The more familiar a hunter is with an area and its deer the better his chances of scoring there. For this reason, some hunters may prefer to hunt locations with low densities of deer over those that have more animals, especially if they don't have time to check out distant spots. Many deer hunters simply don't have as much time to devote to deer hunting as they would like.

Tradition has a lot to do with return trips to familiar deer hunting grounds, too. Over the years the list of fond memories associated with a location grows. Each season then becomes an opportunity to recall past experiences as much as it is an opportunity to have new ones.

35

3

Hunting Regulations

It is surprising how much hunting regulations vary from state to state. What may be legal in one could be illegal in another. Some states prohibit hunting on Sunday, for instance; many others allow it. Variations are also evident on minimum age requirements, hunter safety courses, legal weapons, clothing requirements plus others.

While there are differences in hunting regulations across the country, there are also many that are universal. It is illegal to shoot deer while they are in water or to hunt them with rimfire firearms throughout North America. Legal hunting hours in most areas are a half hour before sunrise until a half hour after sunset. Motorized vehicles, including boats and aircraft, are not permitted to aid in collecting deer. Guns carried in vehicles must be unloaded and cased in most states, too.

Additional regulations relating to weapons that are commonly accepted are: semiautomatic firearms must be restricted to a five-shell capacity; .410 and 28-gauge shotguns are inadequate for deer hunting; nonexpanding bullets are prohibited; and broadheads must be at least 7/8 of an inch wide for deer hunting.

To avoid inadvertently breaking laws relating to deer hunting, hunters should read the guides published by states and provinces they intend to hunt. In Canada handguns are prohibited for deer hunting throughout. Fifty rounds of ammunition can be brought into Canada duty free. Additionally, hunters going into Canada should leave descriptions and serial numbers of their guns with customs officials when entering the country to avoid problems when reentering the U.S. If you can't prove they weren't purchased in Canada, a duty will have to be paid on them.

The following listings will give deer hunters a general idea of some of the regulations and requirements in various states and provinces and Mexico. This information does not represent a total picture of all regulations in any given area, just some of the more pertinent ones that may be useful when planning a hunting trip. Some of those listed may change at any time. Certain counties or management units may have more restrictive regulations than a state or province as a whole. Keep these things in mind when referring to the following listings.

Deer herd estimates, harvests, hunting success percentiles, and addresses of main state or provincial natural resources or fish and game offices plus their phone numbers will be listed in addition to hunting regulations. These are intended to help in planning or preparing for deer hunts. Figures on herd sizes, harvests, and success percentiles are the latest available. They are intended to give hunters a general idea of the hunting situations in each state and province. These figures may vary markedly from year to year.

UNITED STATES

Alabama: This state is not only the first alphabetically, but it also has one of the largest whitetail herds in the U.S. There are an estimated one million. Alabama has the most liberal harvest regulations in the country with one deer a day allowed throughout the season. In a recent year 125,000 deer were harvested.

Centerfire rifles smaller than .240 caliber are not permitted on state-managed areas. Muskets must be .40 caliber or larger. Handguns can be used for deer hunting. Ten-gauge shotguns are also permitted. Some areas permit the use of rifled slugs only in shotguns.

Residents under 16 don't need a hunting license, but must be accompanied by an adult. All nonresident hunters must purchase licenses. Wearing orange is required on wildlife management areas. Dogs may be used for deer hunting.

Department of Conservation and Natural Resources, Information and Education Section, 64 North Union Street, Montgomery 36130 (phone 205-832-6357 or 205-832-6358).

Alaska: Even though the state's blacktail herd isn't large (they number about 100,000), success is high: 60 percent. A recent harvest was 17,000.

Centerfire rifles and handguns are permitted for deer hunting. Shotguns can be 10 gauge maximum. All shotguns are limited to a three-shell capacity. Bows must have a 45-pound pull. Residents under 16 don't need a license. It is illegal to hunt the same day hunters are airborne.

Alaska Department of Fish and Game, Subport Building, Juneau 99801 (907-465-4100).

Arizona: Coues whitetail and mule deer are found in this state. There are about 25,500 of the former and 128,500 of the latter. Hunters harvested over 2,500 whitetails and 10,900 muleys for a combined success of 18.7 percent.

Handguns must be .357 magnum and larger. A 10-gauge, three-shell restriction is in effect. Bows must be at least 40-pound pull.

Hunters under 14 must pass a safety course.

Arizona Game and Fish Department, 2222 West Greenway Road, Phoenix 85068 (telephone 602-942-3000).

Arkansas: Whitetails, 500,000 of them, inhabit this state. Hunters took 27,000 in a recent season for a 10 percent success ratio.

Muzzle-loading rifles must be at least .40 caliber. Handguns of .357 magnum size and larger are permitted with a barrel length of four inches or more.

No license is required for hunters under 16. At least 400 square inches of orange clothing must be worn during gun season. Deer hunters can't set up camp until 48 hours before the season opens.

Arkansas Game and Fish Commission, 2 Capitol Mall, Little Rock 72201 (telephone 501-371-1025).

California: There are 500,000 blacktail deer here, with just under 30,000 taken by hunters recently for 9.2 percent success.

Handgun loads for deer must have a minimum of 695 foot pounds of energy and are only permitted where rifles can be used. Shotguns can hold only three shells and can be 10 gauge. First-time hunters must complete a hunter safety course.

California Department of Fish and Game, 1416 Ninth Street, Sacramento 95814 (telephone 916-445-3531).

Colorado: Approximately 350,000 mule deer roam this state where over 40,000 were bagged by hunters in a season. Those who scored represented 35 percent of the total number of hunters.

Centerfire rifles must shoot a bullet that weighs at least 70 grains and has 1,000 foot pounds of energy at 100 yards. Handguns are not permitted. The 10-gauge, three-shell rule applies, and no buckshot can be used to hunt deer. Muskets must be at least .40 caliber. Bowhunters cannot use mechanical releases.

All persons born after January 1, 1949 must have completed a hunter safety course. Youngsters must be 14 to hunt, and those between 14 and 18 must be accompanied by an adult. At least 500 square inches of orange clothing is required. Deer hunters can only hunt one season per year, either bow, firearms, or muzzle-loading.

Colorado Division of Wildlife, 6060 Broadway, Denver 80216 (telephone 303-825-1192).

Connecticut: Only a little over 500 of this state's estimated 19,000 whitetails were taken by hunters in a recent year for 9 percent success.

There is no Sunday hunting. A small game license must be purchased to apply for a deer permit. A previous license or hunter safety certificate is necessary to be able to hunt. The hunting license must be worn visibly. Individuals under 16 cannot hunt with bow and arrow. Deer kills must be reported.

No rifles can be used for deer hunting, except muskets of .45 caliber and larger with round balls only. Shotgunners are restricted to a three-shell limit and slugs. Hunting arrows must be at least 400 grains in weight, and a bow must be capable of casting an arrow 150 yards.

At least 200 square inches of orange must be worn.

Connecticut Department of Environmental Protection, State Office Building, 165 Capitol Avenue, Hartford 06115 (telephone 203-566-4683).

Delaware: Eleven percent of this state's deer hunters collected whitetails in a season. Approximately 1,500 deer were harvested and the herd size is about 7,000.

Muskets can be .42 caliber and larger. Shotguns can be 10 gauge but can't hold more than three shells. Rifles and handguns are not permitted for deer hunting.

Those under 15 don't need a hunting license but must be accompanied by an adult. Hunters under 18 have to complete a safety course. Four hundred square inches of orange is required. There is no Sunday hunting.

Department of Natural Resources and Environmental Control, Division of Fish and Wildlife, D Street, Dover 19901 (telephone 302-678-4431).

Florida: About 500,000 whitetails call this state home. Four percent of Florida's deer hunters claimed 50,000 in a season.

Centerfire rifles and handguns can be used for deer hunting. Ten-gauge, three-shell limit applies to shotguns. Muskets must be at least .40 caliber.

Dogs are permitted for deer hunting. Evidence of the deer's sex must remain on a carcass.

Florida Game and Fresh Water Fish Commission, 620 South Meridian, Tallahassee 32304 (telephone 904-488-4676).

Georgia: There are whitetails here, 400,000. Deer hunters took 55,000 in a recent year for 10 percent success.

Muzzle-loaders must be .44 caliber or larger. Shotguns must be plugged to hold three shells. Certain centerfire rifles and handguns not permitted for deer hunting are specified in their regulations. Bows must be 40-pound pull or heavier with compounds only to be used in the gun season.

There is no Sunday hunting. Dogs can be used in some areas. Five hundred square inches of orange must be worn and kills must be reported by mail.

Georgia Department of Natural Resources, Trinity-Washington Building, 270 Washington Street S.W., Atlanta 30334 (telephone 404-656-3530).

Idaho: This state has both whitetails and mule deer with the latter in the majority. The estimated population is 218,000 mule deer and 56,000 whitetails. There were almost 21,000 muleys and just over 4,500 whitetails harvested during a past year. Success was 20 percent and 16 percent.

There is a limited number of nonresident permits. Youngsters must be 12 to hunt deer. The evidence of the deer's sex must be left intact on the carcass. Muskets must be at least .40 caliber.

Idaho Department of Fish and Game, 600 South Walnut, P.O. Box 25, Boise 83707 (telephone 208-384-3700).

Illinois: There are about 90,000 whitetails here with a recent harvest of 16,500 and 17.5 percent success.

Deer hunting is for residents only. Shotguns with slugs, .38 caliber and larger muskets, and 40-pound bows and heavier can be used for deer. Deer kills must be reported. Orange clothing is required and licenses must be worn on the back. First-time hunters under 16 must complete a hunter safety course.

Illinois Department of Conservation, Division of Wildlife Resources, 100 East Washington Street, Springfield 62706 (telephone 217-782-6384).

Indiana: Nine percent of Indiana's deer hunters accounted for 9,000 whitetails in a recent season. The estimated herd size is 114,000.

Muskets must be .44 caliber and larger, and slugs are required in shotguns. Centerfire rifles, handguns, and buckshot are prohibited. Bows must have a minimum draw weight of 35 pounds. Mechanical releases are not legal. At least one article of orange must be worn.

Indiana Division of Fish and Wildlife, 608 State Office Building, Indianapolis 46204 (telephone 317-633-7696).

Iowa: Only residents can hunt this state's estimated 50,000 whitetails. Fifteen percent of them scored during a recent year for a tally of over 16,500.

No centerfire guns permitted; muskets must be at least .44 caliber; slugs are required in shotguns. One piece of orange must be worn by gun hunters.

Iowa Conservation Commission, Information and Education, 300 4th Street, Des Moines 50319 (telephone 515-281-5971).

Kansas: Here is another state with both species of deer. There are an estimated 32,000 whitetails and 8,000 muleys. About 4,000 of the former and 1,000 of the latter were bagged by 38.5 percent of the state's residents in a season. Nonresidents can't hunt deer in Kansas.

Centerfire rifles must use bullets at least two inches long, with the exception of the .44. Handguns are not permitted. Muzzle-loaders have to be a minimum of .40 caliber. Bows must be 45-pound pull or heavier.

Hunters must be 16 to try for deer. Persons born after July 1, 1957 must possess a certificate of competency. Use of two-way radios is prohibited for deer hunting. An orange hat plus 200 square inches of orange clothing must be worn. Deer kills must be reported by mail.

Kansas Forestry, Fish, and Game Commission, Box 1028, Pratt 67124 (telephone 319-672-5911).

Kentucky: This state boasts a population of 120,000 whitetails with a harvest of 9,000 and 14 percent success. Centerfire rifles must be .240 caliber and larger. Front-loaders can be .38 caliber and bigger. Slugs in shotguns that are 10 gauge are permitted; buckshot is not. Crossbows are legal here for deer. They must be at least 80 pound. A garment of orange must be worn. All deer kills must be checked with the head intact.

Kentucky Department of Fish and Wildlife Resources, Capital Plaza Tower, Frankfort 40601 (telephone 502-564-4336).

Louisiana: This state's forests harbor about 250,000 whitetails with a harvest of 76,500 and 28 percent success. Centerfire rifles and handguns permitted. Shotguns can be 10 gauge, only three-shell capacity is allowed. Muskets have to be at least .44 caliber. Bows of 30-pound pull and heavier are okay. Dogs are permitted for deer hunting in some areas. Noisy drives are not permitted on management areas. Both archers and gun hunters must wear 400 inches of orange on management units. No permanent tree stands or climbing spurs are allowed.

Louisiana Department of Wildlife and Fisheries, 400 Royal Street, New Orleans 70130 (telephone 504-568-5855).

Maine: Approximately 150,000 whitetails roam this state's woods. There is a harvest of 30,000 deer with 20 percent success. Rifles in .22 magnum rimfire can be used for deer here, handguns are okay and there is a 10-gauge limit on shotguns. Bows must be able to shoot an arrow 150 yards. Orange clothing is required. Persons must be 10 to hunt, and those under 16 must be accompanied by an adult. Nonresidents must be at least 12 to hunt with bow and arrow. Driving deer is illegal in Maine. Sunday hunting is not permitted.

Maine Department of Inland Fisheries and Wildlife, 284 State Street, Augusta 04333 (telephone 207-289-3371).

Maryland: This state's whitetail herd numbers about 70,000 with a harvest of 9,000. There is also a huntable population of sitka deer here. Rifles restricted to certain counties, the same with handguns, which must be .44 magnum. Muskets of .40 caliber and larger are permitted. Bows must have a draw weight of 30 pounds. A hunter safety course is required of first-time hunters. Orange clothing is required. There is no hunting on Sunday.

Maryland Department of Natural Resources, Maryland Wildlife Administration, 580 Taylor Avenue, Annapolis 21401 (telephone 301-269-3195).

Massachusetts: This state has about 13,000 whitetails and a harvest close to 3,000. Shotguns and muzzle-loaders are the only firearms permitted. Muskets must be at least .44 caliber. Forty-pound pull bows are the minimum, and arrows must be labeled with the hunter's name and address. Residents 15 and over need a firearms identification card. Sunday hunting is prohibited.

Massachusetts Division of Fisheries and Wildlife, State Office Building, Government Center, 100 Cambridge Street, Boston 02202 (telephone 617-727-3151).

Michigan: This state is tied with Alabama with a whitetail herd numbering about a million. Fourteen percent of the state's deer hunters claimed 93,000 deer in a season. Persons must be 12 to hunt deer, those from 12 to 16 must be accompanied. Gun hunters must wear orange. Muskets must be .44 or larger. Shotguns only in some counties.

Michigan Department of Natural Resources, P.O. Box 30028, Lansing 48909 (telephone 517-373-1230).

Minnesota: This state has an estimated herd of 400,000 whitetails with a harvest of over 28,500 and 12 percent success. Rifles must be .23 caliber with a shell at least $1^3/_4$ inches long, unless .35 caliber or larger. Muskets must be at least .40 caliber, .45 if they are smoothbores. No handguns permitted. Ten-gauge shotguns are allowed, but no buckshot. Bows must have a minimum draw weight of 40 pounds with 90 to 110 grain broadheads minimum. Persons must be 12 to hunt deer, those under 16 are required to take a hunter safety course. Red or orange clothing is required. Deer hunters can only hunt in the zone stamped on their license. Use of snowmobiles is restricted to certain hours of the day.

Minnesota Division of Fish and Wildlife, 390 Centennial Building, 658 Cedar Street, St. Paul 55155 (telephone 612-296-2894).

Mississippi: Twenty-one percent of this state's deer hunters scored a harvest of 43,600. There are about 300,000 whitetails here. Minimum on muskets is .38 caliber. Orange clothing is required. Dog hunting is permitted. Residents under 16 and nonresidents under 14 don't need hunting licenses.

Mississippi Game and Fish Commission, Box 451, Jackson 39205 (telephone 601-354-7333).

Missouri: There is no estimate on the herd size of this state's whitetails, but 42,900 were harvested in a recent season for 17 percent success. Minimum for handguns and muskets is .357 caliber. Ten-gauge shotguns are okay, and crossbows can be used to hunt deer.

Missouri Department of Conservation, P.O. Box 180, Jefferson City 65101 (telephone 314-751-4115).

Montana: Deer hunters harvest 16,500 whitetails and 26,500 mule deer. Nonresident licenses are limited. Persons must be 12 to hunt, and those under 18 have to have a certificate of competency. At least 400 square inches of orange is required.

Montana Department of Fish and Game, Helena 59601 (telephone 404-449-2535).

Nebraska: Overall success in this state is 53 percent on both whitetail and muleys. There are 50,000 of the former and 35,000 of the latter with harvests of 7,600 and 6,500 respectively. Rifles for deer must have bullets with at least 900 foot pounds of energy at 100 yards. Muskets must be .40 caliber and larger, shotguns can be 10 gauge and are limited to three shells. Handguns are restricted to those of .44, .41, and .357 magnums plus .44 special with magnum handloads. Minimum draw weight for bows is 40 pounds. Deer hunters must be 14, those under 16 have to be accompanied, safety certificates are required of hunters 12 to 15. At least 400 square inches of orange clothing must be worn.

Nebraska Game and Parks Commission, P.O. Box 30370, Lincoln 68503 (telephone 402-464-0641).

Nevada: Mule deer, about 81,500 of them, can be found here. A recent harvest was 5,900 with 35 percent success. Rifle bullets must have 1,000 foot pounds of energy at 100 yards. Front-loaders must be .44 caliber and larger. Handguns must have four-inch barrels and are restricted to .357, .41, and .44 magnums. Bows must be capable of casting a 400-grain arrow 150 yards. Persons must be 12 to hunt. No one under 21 can purchase a license unless he has a previous license or a hunter safety card.

Nevada Department of Fish and Game, Box 10678, Reno 89510 (phone 702-784-6214).

New Hampshire: There are 45,000 whitetails here with a harvest of 9,000 and 10 percent success. Muskets must be .40 caliber minimum, buckshot not permitted in some areas. Bows must be at least 40-pound pull, have arrows labeled, and no mechanical releases are allowed.

Hunters under 17 must possess a certificate of competence. All kills must be reported and deer have to be transported in view.

New Hampshire Fish and Game Department, 34 Bridge Street, Concord 03301 (phone 603-271-3421).

New Jersey: There are approximately 100,000 whitetails here with a harvest just over 13,000 and 6 percent success. No centerfire rifles are permitted, muskets must be a minimum of .44 caliber, shotguns can be 10 gauge but only three shells can be carried in any size scattergun. Minimum draw weight for bows is 35 pounds, and mechanical releases are prohibited. A previous license or completion of a hunter safety course is required. A parent or guardian must apply for licenses for youngsters from 10 to 14. All kills must be registered. There is no Sunday hunting.

New Jersey Division of Fish, Game, and Shellfisheries, P.O. Box 1809, Trenton 08625 (phone 609-292-2965).

New Mexico: A combined harvest of 21,000 deer is achieved for 17.7 percent success here. There are about 18,000 whitetails and 261,000 mule deer. Hunters must choose their weapons here. Minimums are .40 caliber musket, 40-pound bow, and .357 magnum handgun. Safety courses are required for hunters under 18.

New Mexico Department of Game and Fish, State Capitol, Santa Fe 87801 (phone 505 827 2143).

New York: This state boasts a herd of 407,000 whitetails with a harvest of 90,000 and 8 percent success. Rifles and handguns permitted in some areas. Buckshot is not permitted in shotguns, muskets must be at least .44 caliber. Bows must be able to cast an arrow 150 yards, and no mechanical releases are permitted. First-time hunters must complete a hunter safety course. Persons under 16 can't hunt with firearms, but 14-year-olds can hunt with bow and arrow. Sunday hunting is prohibited in parts of the state.

New York Department of Environmental Conservation, Division of Fish and Wildlife, 50 Wolf Road, Albany 12233 (phone 518-457-5690).

North Carolina: About one-third of this state's deer hunters are successful. They harvested just over 53,000 whitetails in a recent season. Herd size is about 500,000. Handguns are not permitted here; rifles can be used only in certain areas; 10-gauge and three-shell limit applies to shotguns; bows must be at least 45-pound pull. Dogs can be used in some areas. There is no Sunday hunting.

North Carolina Wildlife Resources Commission, Albermarle Building, 325 North Salisbury Street, Raleigh 27611 (phone 919-733-3391).

North Dakota: There are four whitetails for every muley in this state. Their populations are 80,000 and 20,000. Harvests are 20,600 and slightly less than 4,000 with 74 and 56 percent success respectively. No handguns permitted; slugs must be used in shotguns; rifles are permitted. Orange clothing required.

North Dakota State Game and Fishing Department, 2121 Lovett Avenue, Bismarck 58505 (phone 701-224-2180).

Ohio: A whitetail herd numbering 100,000 is found here. Success runs about 20 percent with a recent harvest of 25,000. Centerfire rifles and handguns prohibited here; muzzle-loaders of at least .38 caliber can be used; buckshot is not permitted in shotguns. No two-way radios can be used for deer hunting. Persons under 16 must be accompanied by an adult.

Ohio Division of Wildlife, Department of Natural Resources, 1500 Dublin Road, Columbus 43212 (phone 614-466-4630).

Oklahoma: Hunters here have a low success rate: less than 1 percent. There are about 95,000 whitetails in this state with a harvest last year just over 11,500. Centerfire rifles must fire bullets weighing at least 75 grains; buckshot is not permitted; handguns must have barrels at least $3^{1}/_{2}$ inches long and 75-grain bullets that have 500 foot pounds of energy; muskets can be .40 caliber or larger. Five hundred square inches of red, yellow, or orange clothing is required for gun hunters.

Oklahoma Department of Wildlife Conservation, 1801 North Lincoln, Box 53465, Oklahoma City 73105 (phone 405-521-3851).

Oregon: This state has the second largest number of deer in the country. There are blacktails, muleys, and whitetails: 650,000, 400,000, and 4,000 respectively. Whitetails are protected. Harvests of blacktails and muleys are 37,400 and 45,700 with success of 31 and 39 percent. Rifles must be at least .23 caliber, muskets of 40 caliber or larger, 40-pound bows are required. Persons must be 12 to hunt deer; those under 18 must take hunter safety course.

Oregon Department of Fish and Wildlife, 1634 Southwest Alder Street, P.O. Box 3503, Portland 97208 (phone 503-229-5551).

Pennsylvania: This state is tied for fourth in number of deer in the U.S. with 700,000 whitetails. About 150,000 were harvested in a recent season for 15 percent success. Rifles must be .25 caliber or larger, some areas permit shotguns only with buckshot. Bow releases are prohibited. Hunters under 16 must have a previous license or a certificate of competency. Persons must be 12 to hunt deer. No more than 25 hunters can hunt together. Groups of five or more must maintain a roster. Licenses must be worn on the back. Sunday hunting is prohibited. Semiautomatic firearms are not permitted for deer hunting.

Pennsylvania Game Commission, P.O. Box 1567, Harrisburg 17120 (phone 717-787-3633).

Rhode Island: This state probably has the lowest harvest in the country with only about 60 taken during a recent season. Percent success was 2.5 and herd size is 1,500. Shotguns and bows are permitted for hunting. Arrows must be labeled with the hunter's name and address. First-time hunters must pass hunter safety course. Orange clothes are required, 200 square inches. No more than five people can hunt in unison here.

Rhode Island Department of Natural Resources, Division of Fish and Wildlife, 83 Park Street, Providence 02903 (phone 401-227-2784).

South Carolina: Ten percent of this state's deer hunters collected 40,000 whitetails in a season. There are approximately 215,000 deer in the herd. Buckshot is prohibited in some areas; muskets have to be at least .36 caliber. Orange clothing is required. Drives are restricted to the period from 10 A.M. to 2 P.M.; drivers can't carry guns. Heads must not be detached from carcasses. No Sunday hunting is permitted.

South Carolina Wildlife and Marine Resources Department, Division of Game and Fish, Dutch Plaza, Building D, P.O. Box 167, Columbia 29202 (phone 803-758-6524).

South Dakota: A remarkable 81.1 success is obtained here on whitetails and mule deer. There are approximately 90,000 of the former and 75,000 of the latter with harvests of 21,650 and 7,800. Rifle bullets must be at least two inches long; no handguns or buckshot are permitted; muskets must be at least .42 caliber and bows 40-pound pull. Nonresident permits are limited. Applications must be in by July 1. Individuals must be 12 to hunt deer. No more than 20 hunters can be a group for purposes of hunting deer.

South Dakota Department of Game, Fish, and Parks, State Office Building, Pierre 57501 (phone 605-224-3381).

Tennessee: This state has about 180,000 whitetails with a harvest of over 18,000 and 14 percent success. Minimum caliber for centerfire rifles is .24; .40 for front-loaders; handguns must be at least .357 magnum; and bows are required to cast an arrow with at least a 100-

47

grain tip 150 yards. Shotguns must have three-shell capacity and buckshot is not permitted. Orange clothing measuring at least 500 square inches must be worn. Hunter safety courses are required for first-time hunters. Deer applications must be postmarked by August 11.

Tennessee Wildlife Resources Agency, P.O. Box 40747, Ellington Agricultural Center, Nashville 37220 (phone 615-741-1421).

Texas: This state has the largest deer herd in the U.S. There are over three million whitetails and about 150,000 muleys. Almost 300,000 whitetails were harvested in a recent year and 7,600 mule deer. Success runs 46 and 43 percent. Bows must cast arrows 130 yards, and arrows must be labeled with the user's name and address. There is limited dog hunting here. Deer calls are illegal.

Texas Parks and Wildlife Department, John H. Reagan Building, Austin 78701 (phone 512-475-2087).

Utah: There were over 56,600 mule deer harvested here in a recent year with percent success of 34. Muzzle-loaders must be at least .40 caliber; handguns have a .357 magnum minimum; shotguns are prohibited for deer hunting; and bows must have a 40-pound draw weight. Hunters must wear at least 400 square inches of orange. Residents under 21 must have completed a hunter safety course. Hunters must be at least 16 years old.

Utah Division of Wildlife Resources, 1596 W.N. Temple, Salt Lake City 84116 (phone 801-533-9333).

Vermont: Seven percent of this state's deer hunters bagged over 10,200 whitetails last season. Their herd numbers about 160,000. First-time hunters must complete a hunter safety course. Minimum draw weight for bows is 30 pounds.

Vermont Fish And Game Department, Montpelier 05602 (phone 802-828-3371).

Virginia: This state's hunters claimed 63,700 whitetails last year for a success ratio of 21 percent. There are an estimated 300,000 deer in Virginia. Rifle calibers must be a minimum of .23 here; muskets must be at least .45 caliber; shotguns can be a maximum of 10 gauge with three-shell limits; bows must be able to propel an arrow at least 125 yards; handguns are permitted. Slugs are not allowed in some areas where shotguns are required. No Sunday hunting is permitted here.

Virginia Commission of Game and Inland Fisheries, P.O. Box 11104, Richmond 23230 (phone 804-786-4974).

Washington: This state is blessed with blacktails, mule deers, and whitetails with herds of 240,000, 150,000, and 70,000. Harvests are just over 25,000, 17,000, and 6,500 respectively for each type. Success for all three is 22 percent. Muzzle-loaders must be at least .40 caliber; bows must be 40 pounds; no handguns are permitted for deer hunting. Hunters under 18 are required to take a hunter safety course.

Washington Game Department, 600 North Capital Way, Olympia 98504 (phone 206-753-5700).

West Virginia: A herd of 150,000 whitetails occupy this state. Last year's harvest was 35,000 for a 2.5 success ratio. No Sunday hunting is permitted.

West Virginia Department of Natural Resources, Division of Wildlife, 1800 Washington Street East, Charleston 25305 (phone 304-348-2754).

Wisconsin: This state's whitetail herd compares with that of Pennsylvania in size: 700,000. About 136,000 where harvested here last year for a 20 percent rate of success. Minimum caliber for muskets is .40, .45 if a smoothbore is used. Buckshot is not permitted when shotguns are used. Minimum draw weight for bows is 30 pounds. Handguns are not permitted. Deer hunters must be 12 years old. Cap and jacket must be at least 50 percent red, yellow, or orange.

Wisconsin Department of Natural Resources, Bureau of Fish and Wildlife Management, Box 7921, Madison 53707 (phone 608-266-2621).

Wyoming: Deer hunters claim a high success ratio here on muleys and whitetails at 78.8 percent. There are an estimated 280,000 muleys and 51,000 whitetails. Over 61,400 of the former and 14,000 of the latter were harvested in a recent year. Muzzle loaders must be at least .40 caliber; shotguns are required to have a three-shell limit; minimum draw weight on bows is 40 pounds; crossbows are permitted with at least 90 pounds of pull. Hunters must be 14 to try for deer. Orange garments are required for gun hunters. Applications for nonresident permits, which are limited, must be in by March 1. No personal checks will be accepted.

Wyoming Game and Fish Department, Box 1589, Cheyenne 82002 (phone 307-777-7735).

CANADA

Alberta: Whitetails outnumber mule deer two to one in this province. There are 100,000 whitetails. Combined success for both species is 25 percent. Rifles must be at least .23 caliber with bullets measuring more than $1^3/_4$ inches in length. Muskets are required to be a minimum of .44 caliber. Bows must be 40-pound pull or more, and broadheads must be one inch wide. There is a three-shot limit on shotguns. Deer hunters must be 14. A suit and hat of orange or scarlet is required. Most areas prohibit Sunday hunting. Guides are required for nonresidents in some units.

Department of Recreation, Parks and Wildlife, 10363 108 Street, Edmonton T5J 1L8 (phone 403-427-8580).

British Columbia: This province has an estimated 500,000 blacktails, 100,000 mule deer, and 30,000 whitetails. Deer harvest is 29,000 with 40.3 percent success. Shotguns have a two-shell limit here. Recurve or compound bows must draw a minimum of 40 pounds. Crossbows with a 120-pound draw weight are permitted with 250-grain arrows. Nonresidents must hunt with a guide. Proof of completion of hunter safety course is required of first-time hunters.

British Columbia Fish and Wildlife Branch, Department of Research and Conservation, Parliament Buildings, Victoria V8V1X4 (phone 604-387-3091).

Manitoba: Deer season was closed here from 1974 through '76. It was open in 1977. No Sunday hunting is permitted. Bows must draw at least 40 pounds. Deer hunters under 19 must have completed a safety course. A complete suit of white with a blaze orange hat is required.

Department of Renewable Resources and Transportation Services, 1495 St. James Street, Winnipeg R3H 0W9 (phone 204-786-9183).

New Brunswick: This province has an estimated 45,000 whitetails with a harvest of 7,200 for a recent fall. Success varies markedly between resident and nonresident deer hunters. Residents account for 9.7 percent and nonresidents claim 29 percent of the kill. Nonresidents must be accompanied by a guide. There are no special bow seasons here, but archers must use bows with a minimum of 40-pound draw weight. There is no Sunday hunting. Hunters are required to wear at least 400 square inches of orange. Deer must be transported in view and have to be registered.

New Brunswick Department of Natural Resources, Fish and Wildlife Branch, P.O. Box 6000, Fredericton (phone 506-453-2442).

Nova Scotia: This province claims 87,500 whitetails with a kill last fall of 24,000 and 40 percent success. Rifles must be at least .23 caliber; buckshot is not permitted in shotguns that must hold no more than three shells. Bows have to be a minimum of 40-pound pull. Deer hunters 16 years old must have their parent purchase a license for them. Eighteen-year-olds can buy their own. Nonresidents must be accompanied by a resident. There is no Sui day hunting. Drives are illegal here.

Nova Scotia Department of Lands and Forests, Wildlife Division, Box 516, Kentville (phone 902-678-8921).

Ontario: There are an estimated 140,000 whitetails here with a recent harvest of 13,000 and 15 percent success. Rifles in calibers greater than .275 are not permitted in southern Ontario. Shotguns are limited to three shells. First-time hunters under 20 are required to complete a hunter safety course. Fifteen-year-olds can hunt if their parents buy their license; 16-year-olds can buy their own. The Ministry of Natural Resources collects deer hides for tanning.

Ministry of Natural Resources, Parliament Buildings, Toronto M7A 1W3 (phone 416-832-2261).

Quebec: Deer hunters harvested 1,200 whitetails here a year ago. Among rifles prohibited for deer hunting in Quebec are the .30 U.S. carbine, .303 Savage, and .44 magnum. Bows must have a minimum draw weight of 40 pounds. Crossbows are permitted, but must have a draw weight of 80 pounds. A previous license or a hunter safety certificate is necessary to purchase a license.

Quebec Department of Tourism, Fish, and Game, Parliament Buildings, Quebec City G1R 4Y1 (phone 418-643-2256).

Saskatchewan: About 200,000 whitetails roam this province; 32,000 were harvested last fall for a 57 percent success rate. Rifles must be a minimum of .23 caliber. Shotgunners must use slugs. Minimum draw weight on bows is 40 pounds. Arrows are required to have heads one inch wide, and the shafts must be labeled with the hunter's name and address. Hunters must wear an outer suit of white, yellow, scarlet, or orange. There is no Sunday hunting in this province.

Saskatchewan Wildlife Branch, Department of Natural Resources,

Government Administration Building, Regina (phone 306-565-2345), or Sask-Travel, 1825 Lorne Street, Regina (phone 306-565-2300).

MEXICO

Mexico: Both whitetail and mule deer are available here. Hunters who want to try for them will have to provide the government with such necessary information as proof of citizenship; a certificate of good character from their hometown police chief, sheriff, or mayor; a complete description of themselves including name, address, occupation, nationality, height, build, eye color, hair color, and type of forehead, mouth, and chin; firearm descriptions including the amount of ammunition; port of entry; area they wish to hunt; and dates of the hunt.

This information will be necessary to obtain a tourist permit, consular certificate of good conduct, import permit for firearms, and a hunting license. Licenses must be obtained for each state to be hunted in the country. Several recent photographs will be necessary to obtain a certificate of good conduct.

Hunters may bring two rifles with them into the country. They must be smaller than .30-06 caliber. Fifty cartridges can be carried for each gun. Handguns are prohibited.

Hunters interested in hunting in Mexico should study the requirements carefully. More information can be obtained from Dr. Mario Luis Cosia Gabucio, Director General de Fauna Silvestre, S.A.G., Aquiles Serdan No. 28-7 Piso, Mexico 3, D.F., Mexico (phone 905-518-3791).

4

Preseason Scouting

Preseason scouting is one of the most important parts of any deer hunt, whether hunting an area frequented for years or a location being tried for the first time. Granted, preseason checks of familiar hunting grounds need not take as much time as is required to look over new territory. Nonetheless, doing it or not doing it can play a significant role in determining the number of whitetails or muleys that end up on the game pole by the end of the season.

It is not unusual for centers of deer activity to shift from year to year for a variety of reasons. Hunters who fail to detect a change in movement or use patterns before the season opens can lose the most valuable day of hunting of the season: opening day.

Two years ago an uncle of mine found what proved to be a hotspot for bucks on state land. The first day of the season he missed a whitetail with a six- or eight-point rack. A spikehorn he saw the next day wasn't as lucky.

Last season he was all set to go back to the same spot but routinely went to check it out before the season began. It was a good thing he did. A road had been opened in the area and a large field created right where his stand had been. Since there were a few days until opening day he had a chance to locate an alternate position.

This isn't likely to happen on private land, but changes in other factors from year to year such as weather, availability of food, or maturing of the habitat can cause shifts in deer abundance and activity in certain locations.

Something I try to do when scouting territory hunted year after year is to get into pieces of cover I haven't been in before or am not familiar with. This often results in the discovery of new deer hiding places. I often don't get into some of these deer hangouts because they are out-of-the-way or extremely thick. Deer easily find safety in such spots.

Some hunters who hunt the same territory every fall get in the habit of using the same stands, making the same drives, or still-hunting the same course all the time. There is nothing wrong with this, but it often leads to overlooking areas that are worth trying. In addition, deer that live in the vicinity are quick to catch on to the routine and may avoid spots where they have encountered hunters. A change of pace may be the ticket to some easy venison.

When visiting deer country that will be hunted for the first time, hunters should try to look over as much terrain as possible. At the same time they are familiarizing themselves with the deer situation, they are guarding against getting lost. This is a second advantage of preseason scouting in an unfamiliar area.

Along the same lines such features of the terrain that might be mistaken for deer as boulders or stumps can be checked out while scouting. Then hunting time won't be wasted looking at these deerlike objects. This also makes out-of-place shapes that may be deer more noticeable.

Still a third benefit of visiting hunt locations ahead of deer season is the possibility of combining scouting missions with small game hunting. Such small game as squirrels, rabbits, grouse, and other game birds provide action in many states right up to the time some deer seasons begin. Some states may prohibit carrying a gun in the field the week before deer season, however; so be sure it is legal before planning on hunting small game when scouting for deer.

My brother and an uncle collected three Canada geese and a pair of ruffed grouse during a preseason check for deer signs last fall. They bagged more game that day than they often do when intentionally hunting small game or waterfowl. Our luck isn't always that good on scouting trips, but the results of that day are indicative of what can be one of the peripheral benefits of preseason reconnaissance.

The week before deer season opens is usually the best time to scout an area. Starting sooner is a good idea if the location isn't far from where you live and you will be hunting it for the first time. When hunting out of state, scouting must often be restricted to the two or three days before the season, but anything is better than starting cold at the crack of dawn on opening day.

What do you look for when scouting an area for deer hunting? Feed-

This hunter combined small game hunting with scouting for deer. He examines an antler rub while holding ruffed grouse he bagged.

This photo shows a rubbed sapling and a scrape made by a rutting buck. Hunters should look for these signs while scouting.

ing and bedding grounds, regularly used trails, signs of buck activity, and deer themselves are the primary things to keep an eye out for. Water holes should be considered in terrain where water is in short supply. I spend most of my time checking remote locations or those near heavy cover when visiting a new area. This type of terrain invariably get the heaviest use by good bucks throughout the year, but especially once the shooting starts.

I also try to anticipate where other hunters might be while scouting the territory. I prefer not to hunt too near other people, but sometimes it is unavoidable. If I find someone's blind, I go elsewhere in search of a place to hunt.

In open country it is often possible to look over a lot of territory from observation points with the aid of binoculars or spotting scopes. Under these circumstances deer movements can usually be observed. Ani-

I examine well-used deer runway leading into feeding area.

mals that aren't disturbed will generally be found in the same areas once deer season opens.

One fall Dave Raikko and I were hunting mule deer from a drop camp in the Colorado Rockies. We got to our camp a couple of days ahead of the season to look the area over and acclimate to the altitude. The first morning out we located a group of bucks using a patch of willows above timber line. They were still there opening day. We both dropped our deer there that first day of hunting.

Centers of deer activity in wooded terrain can be determined by reading the signs. Trails or runways that receive regular use will usually be well worn. The course of a runway through grass or weeds is marked by a narrow lane of trampled vegetation. Trails through heavily wooded areas will be marked by a line of disturbed leaves that have been scuffed by whitetail or mule deer hooves. Good runways will sometimes be worn right down to the soil in certain spots and tracks can be seen there. Trails are most obvious in sandy areas or when snow is on the ground.

Most regularly traveled trails used by deer are routes they take from bedding to feeding areas and back again. Sometimes animals use different runways going each way. Where water is scarce, trails leading to watering areas are also common. Many times the same network of trails will be used as escape routes. Once a good trail is discovered, feeding and bedding areas can be located by following it both ways. Or, if a feeding area is located, runways leading from it will go to bedding grounds and vice versa if a bedding area is found.

Deer feeding grounds are often openings. For the most part they are agricultural or woodland fields, burned or logged-over areas or orchards. Whitetails and mule deer also feed in locations where there is a lot of low brush and in groves of nut-bearing trees. Groups of deer droppings are common in feeding areas that get regular use.

Deer often bed down in heavy cover or where they have a good view, such as on the sides or tops of hills. Beds are oval-shaped areas where vegetation has been flattened under the weight of the animals. In sand or snow, beds will appear as shallow depressions. Beds can be found next to tree trunks, in rocks, under evergreen boughs, under brush piles or windfalls or in open bogs and in other locations. A number of beds of varying ages will be present in locations used regularly.

Whitetails and muleys generally move from higher to lower elevation or from heavy cover toward openings when feeding and vice versa when retiring. Since deer are the animals they are and their habitats vary from state to state, this isn't always true. I have encountered situations hunting both species of deer when bedding and feeding locations were the same.

In this case deer were concentrated around a cutover area feeding on the downed tops.

Some animals also feed uphill and others travel different trails on a day-to-day basis.

Countless times I've watched muley bucks feed and then lie down in the same patch of cover. It doesn't take brush that is very high to conceal deer. Animals frequently feed for a period of time then lie down out of sight for a couple of hours, then get up and eat some more. They may do this all day and cover very little ground while browsing.

Some of the bigger bucks are least predictable. They often travel routes only used by them and many times don't move during daylight hours when they are vulnerable to hunters. Their normal cautiousness is usually lost during the rut. During this time they frequent areas where does are and travel with them.

Mature whitetail bucks leave telltale signs along the runways they use during the rut. They paw patches of ground that attract does. I believe these scrapes also serve as territorial markers for the benefit of other bucks. Scrapes are often checked at regular intervals by the bucks that made them. Bucks also rub their antlers on trees along trails they use during the rut.

I have seen rubs and scrapes in muley country, too. Since mule deer are not territorial, however, there is no evidence that they return to check scrapes as whitetail bucks do.

Once trails or areas that are being used regularly by deer are located, hunters should try to spend a day or two to determine when deer are using them. Deer use some runways only at night. Hunting these during the day is a waste of time. Watching promising locations from a distance during the hours you will be hunting is the best way to determine if deer will be there and their sex. Try not to alert or alarm deer during this time; it could upset their routine.

Several trails can be checked for use the same day by putting pieces of thread across them at daybreak and checking them a couple of times during the day. Trails where the thread is broken by noon are being used in the morning. Another survey of the trails by dark will show which avenues get use in the afternoon or evening.

Preseason scouting increases the chances of hunters collecting their deer the first couple of days of the season, if done properly, but is no guarantee of such luck. Time and time again when I think I know exactly where to intercept a buck or doe something happens and I draw a blank. Whitetails and muleys simply are not always predictable. With this in mind, try not to forget about scouting once the season opens and even after it closes.

If I have failed to score after several days of sitting at a promising stand, I often combine still-hunting or tracking with a reconnaissance

Scouting territory to find feeding ground and posting along runway leading to it was what helped me collect spikehorn I am holding.

of my surroundings. Sometimes I roam around a little during the middle of each day. This practice has paid off more than once when hunting both whitetails and mule deer. In cases where I have scored and others in my party haven't, scouting during the season has been beneficial in locating more promising territory for them to try.

Tracking deer when snow is on the ground is a surprisingly good way to find out where animals are. Pursued deer often lead trackers to areas where other muleys or whitetails are or have been.

One fall when I scored early in the season and a light covering of snow fell I started tracking deer in an effort to keep them moving, which would increase the chances of my partners getting shooting. The freshest tracks I located one morning were of a doe and her youngster. I tailed them for several hours and they led me to a patch of high ground surrounded by thick, lowland swamp. There were a lot of buck signs there.

We didn't get a chance to hunt there that year, but we did following seasons. Between my brother and me we have taken four bucks and missed a couple of others on that isolated patch of high ground. One of them is my best whitetail to date.

Another cold, snowy day I took a walk to a partner's stand at noon to warm up. I hadn't seen a thing. George saw one deer at a distance and was unable to tell if it was a buck or doe. I tracked the animal for a while and it led me through an area with a heavily used runway.

Hunters should also keep an eye open for deer while scouting. If these mule deer aren't disturbed before the season opens they should be in the same area.

Three of us posted in that vicinity the next morning. An eight-point buck walked by me shortly after daylight. I missed it, but he made the mistake of running into my brother. Bruce downed him.

Postseason scouting can be valuable for hunting in the same area the next year. During the course of a hunting season deer frequently change their travel patterns as well as their bedding and feeding grounds. Whitetails and mule deer generally react to hunting pressure the same way each season. Learning which trails animals in your area use most once the shooting starts can help determine how to connect quickly the next fall.

It is difficult to do too much scouting for deer. Something new about whitetail or muley behavior is often learned each trip. The more hunters know about deer in the area they hunt, the better their chances are of collecting one there consistently. That is what scouting is all about.

5

Stand Hunting

Patience is one of the most difficult and important attributes for a deer hunter to master. It can prove the difference between success and failure in most whitetail or mule deer hunting methods.

Patience is especially rewarding for the stand hunter, hours or days may pass before a buck is sighted. But determined vigilance on a stand often pays off; in fact, stand hunting probably accounts for more downed deer in the fall than any other method.

The reasons for this success are easy to understand. Two of the more commonly used techniques available to solitary hunters, still-hunting and tracking, match pursuer and pursued on a one-to-one basis. The average deer hunter's senses and stealth in the field are simply no match for those of his quarry.

Hunting from a properly chosen stand places all the advantages in the hunter's favor. In a stationary position the sitter's strongest senses, sight and hearing, can be utilized to the fullest. At the same time, the effectiveness of a deer's faculties in detecting a hunter will be impaired.

By being downwind of where animals are expected to appear, the hunter's scent will often go undected. The use of natural cover or a properly constructed blind to conceal himself combined with minimal movements will reduce his visibility to a deer. With little or no movement unnatural sounds are avoided, and a deer is not likely to hear the hunter.

Hunting from a stand can be productive most hours of the day and under most weather conditions. This is another factor in the technique's favor. The circumstances in which a stand hunter would be least likely to see game is during stormy weather, when both deer and hunter activity are at a minimum

On most days during the fall, animals will travel to and from feeding areas or their reproductive drive will keep them on the move. Where hunting pressure is heavy, the vulnerability of deer to stand hunters is increased. Plenty of hunters in the woods are bound to keep the deer stirred up and increase the likelihood of trail watchers seeing game.

Basically, stand hunting can be broken down into a sequence of four steps: selecting sites, preparing them for the hunt, hunter preparation, and procedure once in position.

Preseason work and scouting is important for successful stand hunting. Three of the four points mentioned above should be looked after before opening day. Far too many hunters waste opening day by not having any idea where they want to be once shooting time begins, or they spend the first few critical hours fixing up a stand decided on the night before. The bulk of the States' deer harvest occurs the first few days of the season, especially in heavily hunted whitetail country. A hunter who doesn't take advantage of every minute of the first few days is drastically reducing his chances of success.

Ideally, scouting activity should be concentrated one to two weeks before deer season begins. That way a hunter will get a handle on current conditions. Deer concentrations and movements can vary greatly from one month to the next. A shift in habits will often accompany a weather change. As an example, deer will move differently when snow is on the ground than when it is bare.

Without snow covering the landscape, whitetails and muleys blend into their surroundings fairly well, even in relatively open terrain. With a white backdrop of snow in open to semiopen country, deer stand out in stark contrast to their surroundings. They seem to sense their increased visibility to hunters under these circumstances and move into timber, swamps, or brush.

There is a swampy swale in Michigan that either my brother or I have taken a whitetail buck from the first couple days of the season for several years. Tag alders grow thick in the swale along with tall marsh grass, which provides plenty of concealment for whitetails. There was never snow on the ground when we met with success in that spot.

One year we had an early snowfall, and the ground was snow-covered the first week of the season. My brother sat in that swale for two days without seeing a single deer. Because of the snow, visibility was about three times greater than normal. The alders didn't look as dense as they did without snow, and the marsh grass was matted down.

Whitetails that normally traveled through that swale were probably using an alternate route through evergreens where they would be less conspicuous.

Sometimes the available cover itself will undergo a change, which will cause deer to adjust their travel patterns. A prime example is leaf fall from deciduous trees such as maple, beech, birch, oak, and aspen.

One fall when I was hunting mule deer in Colorado a heavy rain combined with strong wind practically defoliated all of the quaking aspens in my area overnight. Before that time my party had been seeing muleys in the quakies on a regular basis. After the leaves came down most of the deer moved into the surrounding timber.

If the time isn't available to visit the hunt area a week or two ahead, it is advisable to set up camp at least two days before the season opener. An early arrival has other advantages in addition to allowing time for scouting; you can also set up camp or arrange motel accommodations at a leisurely pace. Last minute arrivals and the corresponding hassles which often arise can overtax your system and reduce productivity during the hunt.

If preseason scouting isn't possible, secure a guide who will do it for you. One who knows the habits of the deer in his area can be a distinct advantage. Guides will be discussed in greater detail in chapter 14.

The most important procedure in successful stand hunting is selecting a spot to wait for deer to show. Not only must the hunter consider the animals' normal movement patterns, but he must also try to anticipate how the deer will react to hunting pressure; unless he or she is in one of those rare locations where few other deer hunters tread. Otherwise, competing hunters' density and points of access are of prime concern.

Step number one in selecting a stand site is to become familiar with the locality that will be hunted by learning the lay of the land. County and topographic maps come in handy for deciding on an area that might be suitable for hunting. Try to isolate one chunk of terrain at a time. One square mile, or less, of country is plenty to work with. In many cases a 40-acre plot is enough. Territory completely surrounded by roads is easily defined. In many cases, however, a fence, river or creek, lake, ridge or transition zone from one type of cover to another will have to be chosen as a boundary.

Once a feeling for the lay of the land is obtained on paper, get out there on foot with a compass. Walk as much of it as possible to familiarize yourself with the various cover types present and the basic features of the terrain. At the same time, you will be guarding against getting lost by becoming familiar with the tract.

While familiarizing yourself with the terrain keep an eye out for deer. Any signs of them, such as feeding and bedding areas or trails, are worthy of note.

Check trails after a rain to be sure they are receiving regular use. Or tie a piece of thread across the trail, one to two feet off the ground, early in the morning. If the thread is broken by nightfall the trails were traveled during the day. Another way is to spend a day before the season in your stand (without a weapon, of course).

If, after scouting an area, you aren't satisfied with what you found—not many deer signs, too many roads, or some other displeasing factor—pick out another locality. Keep it up until finding circumstances you will be happy with. This is the advantage of beginning preparations well in advance of the season opening. If not enough time is allotted for scouting by a hunter, he may end up hunting in a location with which he isn't completely satisfied.

Incidentally, a high density of deer isn't necessary in an area to be able to score from a stand. It's just a matter of being able to intercept one animal. Proper scouting is the key to accomplishing this.

In the northern counties of the Upper Peninsula of Michigan, which border Lake Superior, winters are long and severe and winter deer range is poor. As you would expect, deer densities are low. Nonetheless, my brother, an uncle and I managed to collect at least one whitetail buck a year (one season we got two) among us from a spot within sight of the big lake for a number of years running.

The location we hunted was a series of rugged hills that dropped off to lowland swamps on two sides. On preseason scouting trips the first year we hunted there we learned what runways whitetails used to get into the hills from the lowlands. When other hunters moved the deer out of the swamps on opening day at least one of us would drop a buck.

Once the lay of the land and areas of heaviest deer use have been pinpointed, choosing specific stands should be a simple matter. As a general rule, it is better to situate yourself closer to bedding areas than feeding grounds. There are exceptions to this that I will get to shortly. The odds of seeing animals in these localities are best during daylight hours. Whitetail and mule deer often reach resting areas after daylight and leave before dark.

In addition, bedding grounds are usually in heavy cover or higher in elevation than feeding areas. Deer disturbed during any hour of the day by moving hunters commonly seek thick cover or gain altitude to escape; so they are apt to move your way.

Stand hunters will have their best chance at big bucks once the rut starts. They are more active during daylight hours than otherwise. This buck's swollen neck is a sign that he is in the rut *(photo credit: Bob Landis)*.

During firearms seasons, deer often use the same escape routes year after year, roads that lead to exceptionally heavy cover or relatively inaccessible country. If you know where such a trail is from past experience in your territory, posting along it could be productive.

Early in the fall, primarily during bow seasons, picking a stand near feeding areas may be better than locating close to bedding grounds, at least for hunting during evenings. Deer often start feeding before it gets dark then. Where it is legal, some hunters bait deer with foods such as apples, corn, and potatoes.

If you are looking for a buck with a decent rack or if there is expected to be a high density of hunters in your area, it may be advisable to head for the remotest parcel of your scouted acreage. The harder a location is to reach, the better the chances mature bucks will be in residence. A large influx of hunters will usually push additional deer into remote sections as well.

Big bucks are easier to locate once the rut has started. Moss-horned muleys will leave elevated haunts and go to lower areas in search of does. Both species of bucks are also more active during daylight hours when they are looking for does.

When the rut is on, whitetail hunters should try to pick a stand overlooking a series of scrapes. The branch this hunter is looking at was broken by the buck that pawed the ground underneath it.

Deer hunters who find a tree this large that has been rubbed by a buck will be in the territory of a trophy animal.

Antlered whitetails mark their territory with scrapes or pawings. These are patches of ground from one foot to four feet across that have been pawed clear of leaves and other debris. Antler rubbings are small trees that have been rubbed free of bark on one side by bucks polishing their antlers.

Buck signs are usually noted while scouting. Bucks periodically check their network of pawings, and being located along a trail marked with scrapes can put you on the way to success. Here again, pick a spot in or near heavy cover. There is more of a chance a buck will cruise that stretch during daylight hours. Scrapes in open areas will, most likely, be saved for after dark.

Search out migration trails for a late-season stand. Once snow flies, mule deer head from mountains down to valleys; whitetails, in some locations, move toward yarding areas, which are often expansive lowland swamps. The animals generally follow the same trails to winter quarters every winter.

Consider prevailing wind currents when selecting specific sites for stands. You want to be downwind of where deer will appear. When in hilly country, remember that air currents rise in the morning and flow downhill in the evening. It may be advisable to watch a runway from up the slope early in the day and move to a vantage point below the trail later in the day.

Wind directions vary from day to day, and it is a good practice to have alternate stands to cover a hot trail. Going one step further, a wise hunter will select one or two backup spots for stands before the season, separated by a quarter mile or more, in the event his first choice doesn't pan out for some reason. This way there is no great loss of valuable time in relocating.

Another consideration in stand location is never to situate yourself where you can keep an eye on everything. Being able to see one well-used travel route or the junction of two runways is plenty. Also, stay within a reasonable shooting distance off to the side of the trails. This distance will vary, depending upon the terrain hunted. In brush country it may be only 30 yards, while in open areas it may be from 100 to 150 yards.

Once you've decided on one or several spots for stands, some cover will be necessary to break your outline while standing. There are three options available: using a natural cover, building a blind, or using an elevated platform, where legal. Natural cover is preferable whenever available.

Clumps of brush, fallen trees, large rocks, and low-hanging boughs of evergreen trees usually do the job. However, don't restrict freedom of movement and your visibility for concealment. It will do little good to be so well hidden from a buck that a good shot is impossible. Many times hunters are so screened they can't see the deer until it is too late.

When you are building blinds, try to use materials available nearby, such as dead limbs, pine boughs, etc. If other materials are lacking, camouflage netting or burlap can be used to fashion a blind.

One way to use netting is to wrap it around two or three trees that are close together. Sticks, stakes, brush, or bushes can also serve as a framework to attach the material to around the chosen stand site. Here again, never construct a covering that obscures sight, sound, or maneuverability.

A blind should be erected at least a week before the season; so local animals will grow accustomed to it. A blind erected the day before the season is bound to make every nearby deer wary of your position.

This deer hunter is taking advantage of an existing situation for his stand rather than constructing a blind. The stump behind him serves as a backrest and also breaks his outline. A log is used as a seat. A cushion and pine boughs make it more comfortable.

Whether using natural cover or building a blind, a backrest and comfortable seat will make the vigil more bearable, which is necessary to be able to stay in place for any length of time. Stumps or tree trunks serve well as backrests and can be used in conjunction with a log, boat cushion, or collapsible stool. A folding lawn chair is best of all if carrying it in isn't a problem. Placing it in position before the season can be an advantage.

A variation of the ground blind that isn't used by many deer hunters, but is effective, involves digging a pit, either circular or rectangular. The best position for a pit blind is on the slope or crest of a hill. When on level ground, brush and small mounds easily obstruct a hunter's view. A hatchet and shovel will be necessary to dig a satisfactory hole because roots are often encountered during the excavation process.

Circular pit blinds resemble a thermos bottle cap, stopper down, from the side. The upper portion of the hole should be about six feet across and three feet deep. It should be deep enough for all but a hunter's head to be out of sight when he is sitting down. Another smaller hole (about three feet wide) is then dug in the center of the first one to make a space for legs. With this design a hunter can sit facing any direction.

Squared-off pit blinds are also constructed with two levels; so it is possible to sit comfortably in them. Sides of the pit serve as a backrest.

This type can be constructed to allow sitting at one or both ends of the pit. These can be six feet long and half as wide.

Dirt removed from holes can be distributed around the outside edge and should be covered with leaves or brush after the job is completed. Pine boughs can be used to cover a portion of the pit, just leaving enough room to sit. This protects foxhole hunters from cold. The side of the pit hunters will be leaning against can be covered with plastic to keep their backs dry. A boat cushion is comfortable to sit on.

Check to make sure this practice is permissible whether you are hunting on private or public land.

Elevated stands (where legal) are popular for deer hunting in wooded locations. With their use, hunters can get above their quarry's normal line of sight and escape detection in this manner. Whitetails and muleys do not expect danger from above and seldom look up, unless alerted by an out-of-place noise. Additionally, deer are less likely to wind a hunter in an elevated position.

While trying for a mule deer one fall in Wyoming with bow and arrow, I started out the day from a stand on the ground. Wind currents were finicky that day. For a time it would be blowing one direction; then it would shift for 15 minutes before changing again. Since it was morning, the general flow of air was uphill; so I chose a position on the uphill side of where I expected deer to show.

Several groups of does passed by at a distance; then a buck began working toward me. He was feeding uphill and the wind was in my favor. When that muley buck was 20 yards away and I was about to draw, the wind shifted. He scented me and wasted little time getting out of there.

After that episode I found a tree with sturdy limbs to stand on about 15 feet off the ground and continued my vigil. Within a half hour another buck showed and came within 25 yards, where I arrowed him. Switching wind notwithstanding, that buck didn't know I was there.

In areas where permanent tree stands are permitted, those constructed of fresh lumber should be spray-painted with green, brown, or black to reduce the boards' visibility. Injuring trees by installing stands with nails is prohibited in many states. In these locations portable stands are the best choice.

When nails are used to install a tree stand, they should be removed when the platform is removed. Nails left in a tree can ruin a saw if the tree is ever cut.

Few tree stand hunters take the time to consider a tree's market value as lumber or pulp, but they should. If possible, only use portable or permanent elevated stands in trees with low market value. If you

This bowhunter takes advantage of a couple of sturdy limbs to serve as a tree stand.

don't know the difference between high-quality and low-quality trees, a visit with a local forester can be worthwhile.

Commercially manufactured, portable tree stands are becoming increasingly popular because of their versatility. Some, such as the model made by Baker Manufacturing Company, P.O. Box 1003, Valdosta, Georgia, come complete with a climbing tool. Changing stand sites with portable tree stands can be accomplished in a matter of minutes.

Shiny metallic surfaces on portable tree stands should be dulled by covering them with paint. Green, black, brown, or a combination of these colors work well.

Lacking a platform, some hunters simply utilize a convenient crotch in a tree with ample space to get comfortable. For maximum benefit, an elevated hunter should be about 30 feet above the ground. Sometimes getting this high isn't possible, in that case 12 to 15 feet off the ground will do.

Additionally, a tree stand should be located on the side of a tree opposite a deer trail. In this position there is less likelihood a deer will see the hunter. This is an especially useful tip for bowhunters. The movement an archer makes when drawing his bow sometimes attracts a deer's attention. When on the opposite side of a tree trunk, there is less chance of this happening.

All tree stand hunters should be safety conscious when climbing into position. There is always a possibility of injuring yourself or damaging equipment in the event of a fall. The best practice is to raise and lower a weapon from a tree with a rope. Archers should have all broadheads in a covered quiver. Rifles and shotguns should be empty when brought up or lowered from a tree.

It is also advisable to use a safety harness while hunting from a tree stand. The belt or rope guards against the hunter's falling from his perch if he gets drowsy or loses his balance.

The next step in readying a stand is to clear away all forest litter within five feet of where you will be positioned if you are on the ground. A nervous foot crunching dead leaves for the ground-based stand hunter won't do much for keeping his presence a secret. This is also a precaution in case he has to stand up to stretch cramped muscles or try to get a better look at a deer.

Along the same lines, bothersome branches and twigs that may restrict your view or bump your weapon when raising or swinging it should be removed where you will be sitting or standing. Check all quadrants—front, sides, and back—by shouldering or drawing and swinging your weapon.

Limbs that are trimmed should be cut flush with tree trunks rather than leaving stubs that are several inches long. Stubs of limbs will eventually die and fall off, which reduces the quality of the tree for lumber. When the stubs fall off they will leave holes in the wood.

A hunting companion of mine didn't get a shot at what he guessed was a ten-point whitetail buck one year; because he failed to remove twigs that might be in his way on all sides. He was sitting with his back against a stump when he heard something walking behind him. It was making so much noise he thought it had to be another hunter. When my partner peeked around the stump he saw the big buck. He slowly brought his rifle around and up to take a shot. When the gun was halfway to his shoulder, the barrel hit a twig and the twig snapped off. That buck was gone in less time than it takes to tell about it.

Once interfering brush and limbs are removed, a bowhunter should consider pacing the distance from his stand to various points where shots at deer can be expected. Archers who don't know how long a step they take should measure it in order to gauge yardages accurately. It is important that bowhunters know how far a deer is when they fire. Unlike bullets, arrows drop fast. A five- or ten-yard mistake in estimating distance can make the difference between a hit and a miss. Sticks can be stuck in the ground to mark various yardages. Most of the time, however, trees, brush, rocks, and other natural features that are already present will serve as satisfactory distance markers.

There is one more step in preparing a stand for the hunt. Since you want to be seated before first light, if possible, and stay until shooting light has faded, be sure you will be able to find your way in and out from your post by flashlight. If you can do it with no aids, all the better. Consider marking some sort of a trail if you can't find your stand unaided.

Fluorescent tape is handy for marking trees. In some cases blaze marks can also be used. Don't designate your route from where you leave your car all the way to your stand, however. Only use guideposts where necessary. Otherwise, you may have a number of curious hunters visiting during the day.

Proper mental attitude is involved in preparing yourself for the hunt. Mentally, you have to convince yourself that your post is the best position available in your area. Be confident and tell yourself that by sticking it out you will eventually get a chance for a shot. Staying put for only a few hours isn't enough. Unless, of course, you score quickly. A quick score can happen, but don't count on it. Plan on spending the entire day in your spot if possible. If you can only handle a few hours at a time, spend the first few hours of the day, midday, and the last couple of hours in position. Most kills occur during those time periods.

Going hand in hand with a proper mental attitude is a good night's sleep. Don't stay up until all hours playing cards with the guys or drinking. A groggy mind can't be enthusiastic about anything.

The last point to consider is how to wait. Sounds simple enough, but there are a few points worth mentioning. Always be alert and ready to shoot. Listen for sounds and look for movements. Keep your gun, bow, or camera on your lap or gripped in your hands ready to shoulder, draw, or raise it.

If at all possible, don't wear earmuffs or a hood since these will affect your ability to see or hear a deer approaching.

After a time, familiarity will develop for how everything looks and sounds in the immediate vicinity. More often than not, anything out of the ordinary will be noticed immediately. Keep looking all around you, moving the head slowly from one side to the other.

Keep your personal noises to a minimum. Wrap food in material that isn't exceptionally noisy. Shifting positions regularly to maintain comfort is unavoidable. Always stay alert while doing it.

As far as smoking is concerned, if you are situated downwind from

To be sure you will be able to find your stand before daylight it is a good idea to mark a trail to it. This hunter is using blaze marks on trees as trail markers.

where deer are going to be they probably won't notice it. Whitetails and mule deer are apt to notice the movements associated with smoking, however; so it is best to smoke as little as possible.

Scents designed to mask a hunter's odor will have little impact on hunting success if his stand is downwind of where deer are expected to show. When air currents are constantly shifting or deer approach from an unexpected direction they can be advantageous. Try to use a scent that is natural for the area being hunted. Deer gland or skunk musk scents are the most versatile. Bucks may be attracted to scents made from glands of does if the rut is on. Opened bottles of scent can be posi-

73

tioned in an elevated position at the hunter's stand or applied to a strategically placed ball of cotton.

There are plenty of things to keep your mind occupied while you wait. Observing birds and animals, other than deer, can be entertaining. Sometimes they will warn you of an approaching deer. Every time a jay squawks or a squirrel chatters, you should wonder why.

A nearby shot, the snap of a twig, or the rustling of leaves may mean a deer is coming your way. Look for and identify the source of every sound.

I collected a nice 10-point mule deer in Colorado one fall by paying attention to rifle shots in my area. When I heard a group of shots over a ridge from me I knew that hunters had jumped some game and, if the shooters didn't connect, the animals should come uphill over the ridge. I kept my eyes glued on the skyline.

Within five minutes, not one, but seven bucks came over the top and into my lap. The ten-pointer I dropped was the biggest of the bunch.

Once the whitetail or mule deer is sighted, get ready as quickly as possible. If you are sure a deer is approaching by sound, get your weapon up. That's one less movement you'll have to make when it comes in sight. If deer catch you offguard and are visible before you hear them, don't move, unless the animal you want is on the move and will be out of sight shortly. Take the first decent opportunity for a shot when the buck has his head down or is looking the other way.

When that antlered deer goes down, you will be a confirmed stand hunter. Hunting in that fashion may take a lot of time, work, and patience, but it will be worth it when you walk over and inspect that buck.

6

Still-hunting and Stalking

Still-hunting and stalking are difficult to separate; the same basic skills are required for each. The major difference is that while stalking, a deer hunter already has his quarry in sight. A still-hunter is searching for deer, but he may become a stalker as soon as he spots a whitetail or mule deer that must be approached before a shot is possible.

Still-hunting requires more activity than stand hunting. The hunter is on the move, but not constantly. When he is moving, it is at a very slow pace. A still-hunter actually takes many stands during a hunt, but he occupies each one for brief periods of time compared to the duration a dedicated stand hunter often remains in one spot.

Normally, a hunter using the stop-and-go technique only remains motionless for a matter of minutes; but on occasion, he will stay in place for as long as half an hour. It depends on the circumstances.

Stalking is simply a matter of decreasing the distance between a hunter and his quarry without being detected. The acceptable range depends on the weapon a hunter is using and his ability with it. A bow-hunter, for instance, may want to get within 50 yards of his target; a musket hunter or shotgunner might consider 100 yards his maximum range; and a rifleman using a .270 might feel confident of dropping a deer between 200 and 300 yards.

Obviously, deer hunters who use primitive weapons or shotguns will have to be more skillful at stalking than hunters who use modern rifles. Where open country is common, as it is in many of the western states, stalking ability can be an important skill to rifle hunters as well.

Still-hunting and stalking can be employed successfully in most covers and terrains and under varying conditions. The only cover where these methods aren't practical is where visibility is 50 yards or less. Vegetation in these locations is often too dense to permit moving stealthily, and any deer in the area will be long gone before a hunter can see them.

Stop-and-go hunting can be practiced most effectively in territory a hunter is familiar with. Knowledge of prime bedding and feeding areas and preferred travel routes allow a still-hunter to make the most of wind, terrain, and his ability. When planning on still-hunting unfamiliar country, try to scout the area as thoroughly as possible before the season opens.

Contrary to what some hunters believe, still-hunting is not a technique that goes hand in hand with covering long distances and lots of terrain, especially in typical whitetail and blacktail habitat or when searching for muleys in timber. Covering a distance of 100 yards can take an hour. Where visibility is a couple hundred yards or more, a still-hunter may travel further than he would in denser cover. Not a great deal more, however, because he should spend correspondingly more time carefully looking over every place a deer might be.

Still-hunting is not a casual approach to collecting a deer, either. Practicing it properly takes a lot of concentration, at least it does for me. I have to remind myself at regular intervals to move slowly and search every inch of the area around me. If I start daydreaming and forget about what I'm supposed to be doing, my pace automatically quickens and my eyes start bouncing from one view to the next with casual glances rather than the thoroughness necessary in still-hunting.

Admittedly, I'm not the best still-hunter. Nonetheless, I've taken a number of deer while hunting this way and have seen many more that got away. One advantage stop-and-go hunting has over hunting from a stand is that more deer are usually seen. But many of them are no more than flashes or waving tails.

The skills inherent in still-hunting can become second nature with practice. I've watched some still-hunters who are old hands at the technique and are regularly successful. Their movements are as instinctive and stealthy as the deer they hunt.

Beryl Jensen, a fellow Michigan deer hunter from Marquette, is a perfect example of a skillful still-hunter. We made arrangements to meet at my stand late in the morning one day. My post was in an old burn, and Beryl would have to cross an opening about 100 yards across to reach the spot.

I was watching for him as well as keeping an eye out for deer. When

Beryl arrived, he appeared as suddenly as deer often do. He was a full 20 to 30 yards into the opening before I noticed him. I watched him closely as he approached.

It looked as if he floated across the remaining distance. He would take several short steps then pause and look around. The movement his legs made was almost imperceptible. I'm sure he saw me as soon as he entered the opening, but he advanced at his normal stop-and-go hunting pace. If there had been any deer in the vicinity, his presence certainly wouldn't have spooked them.

There are no hard-and-fast rules designating the perfect still-hunting pace. The terrain, visibility, ground cover and condition, and weather will dictate to some degree how to proceed. Each hunter will probably develop his own variations in pace.

As a general rule, taking from three to five steps between pauses is about right. Each advancement often brings a new area into view or gives the still-hunter a different perspective on a piece of cover looked at minutes before. Try to check each shadow, clump of trees, brush, or tall grass carefully with your eyes. Deer can blend in surprisingly well with their surroundings.

Try to remember to look in all directions, behind as well as in front and to the sides. A still-hunter shouldn't move his head in quick, jerky movements, but in a slow, rotating motion. Also try to keep in mind the importance of focusing on the terrain as far ahead as possible. Don't expect deer to wait until you are almost on top of them. Their senses are keener than yours. To increase the chances of seeing them before they see, smell, or hear you, look as far ahead as possible.

Don't expect to see an entire animal. Try to pick out the deer's ears, legs, antlers, tail, or the horizontal lines along the back or belly. Subtle movements like a twitching ear or swishing tail can give a muley's or whitetail's position away, too. Once you home in on a part of an animal, the rest of its body will usually jump into focus, unless it is obscured.

If the deer that is spotted isn't the one you want, keep looking. There may be others with it, either to the sides or behind it. If you haven't been detected, try to remain motionless as long as possible, unless moving won't disturb the animal. Other deer will probably give themselves away eventually.

An effort should be made to get by deer that the hunter isn't interested in without spooking them. An alarmed deer may alert others in the vicinity.

When the rut is on and several does are encountered it can be worthwhile to watch them or where they were for at least a half hour, on the

A buck will often follow a doe or two as shown here when the rut is on. Be sure to wait long enough, as much as a half hour sometimes, after seeing a doe. Many times a buck will be some distance behind *(photo credit: Scott Stewart).*

chance a buck might trail them. I blew what could have been a perfect chance at a whitetail buck one time by not waiting long enough after seeing a doe.

I had stopped and was checking the cover ahead of me when the doe walked into view from left to right about 60 yards away. When she went out of sight I got down in a sitting position with my rifle at ready on the chance a buck was following her. Nothing happened for several minutes; so I got up and slowly walked toward where the doe had been. When I reached her tracks there was a snort off to my left as a buck whirled and hightailed it. There wasn't enough time for a shot.

Hearing is important to still-hunters, too. A hunter who hears a nearby noise he can't identify should pause until he determines its source. The same goes for an unidentified movement. The disturbance may have been caused by a flitting bird or a nervous squirrel, but there is always the chance a deer is at the root of it. Patience often provides the best means for a still-hunter to discover the source of what attracted his attention.

Some of the deer a still-hunter sees will be running, having been spooked by his presence or other hunters. These shots should be passed up, unless the animal's sex can be determined and there is an opportunity to put a bullet in a vital area.

There are several things to keep in mind while still-hunting that can increase the chances of getting standing shots. Scent, sight, and sound, or the lack of them, are the three major factors that will make a difference. It is best to stop-and-go hunt into the wind. This eliminates the possibility of any deer ahead of a hunter smelling him. A moderate to strong wind will also cover up some of the noise made by a still-hunter while walking.

Hunting across the wind is alright, too. Deer ahead of the hunter still won't be able to wind him, nor will those on his upwind side. Any whitetails or muleys on the downwind side should be spotted before they are able to scent a hunter traveling across the wind.

A still-hunter's movement can be kept to a minimum if he takes short steps and swivels his head slowly. His visibility can be reduced by wearing camouflage clothes when possible. Additionally, still-hunters should avoid exposing themselves in the open by walking through fields or skylining themselves on ridges. Try to skirt the edge of fields and openings. When crossing a ridge, keep a low profile.

Still-hunting along a ridge can often be productive since deer don't usually expect danger from above and elevation gives the hunter an excellent view of the surrounding terrain. It is better, however, to walk just below the ridge top rather than directly on top.

The amount of noise a still-hunter makes or doesn't make is a func-

Still-hunting in such a way that the hunter is above any deer he expects to see is as advantageous as when hunting from a stand, but try not to be silhouetted against the sky.

When snow blankets the ground, it is one of the quietest conditions for stillhunting.

tion of how light-footed he is, how thick the cover is, and how his clothes are made. The way a still-hunter walks can be just as important as how much he walks. Hunters should try to walk with most of their weight either on the heel or ball of the foot. Either portion of the foot should touch the ground first, then the rest of the foot can be lowered. This, in effect, reduces the surface area making initial contact with the ground, thereby reducing noise.

Still-hunters should also try to lift their feet clear of noisy ground cover rather than dragging their heels or shuffling their feet.

Outer garments of wool are the quietest clothes for deer hunting in cool to cold weather. Cotton is a quiet fabric, too, but since it isn't as warm as wool it can be worn comfortably in warmer weather.

Ground cover and conditions can have a significant impact on the effectiveness of stop-and-go hunters. Quietest ground conditions are grass, sand, and solid rocks, after a soaking rain or when the forest floor is blanketed with soft snow or pine needles. Still-hunting can be excellent under any of these circumstances. The technique is also worth trying in a strong wind, regardless of the ground conditions. Disturbance created by gusty winds is often enough to drown out noises a hunter might make.

One noise hazard stop-and-go hunters should always be mindful of are brittle twigs and sticks that are sometimes hidden under leaves or snow. Try to avoid snapping these when you walk, but don't spend so much time watching where your feet are going that any deer up ahead might go unseen. If a twig is broken it is a good idea to stop for a few minutes and then continue on.

Dry leaves, crunchy snow, and loose rocks are the worst conditions to still-hunt in. Even in these noisiest of situations the stop-and-go method can be productive. Noise, in itself, doesn't alert deer, but the cadence or frequency will. Many hunters walk at a consistent pace. Animals pause frequently when traveling.

Muleys and whitetails know the difference. When they hear a stop-and-go hunter approaching they are apt to be more curious than afraid. As a result, they are likely to stay put and offer a shot. Deer and hunters are at an equal disadvantage when conditions are noisy since each can hear the other better than usual.

Still-hunters can reduce the amount of disturbance they make under

Paddling a canoe on a river or stream is a perfect way to still-hunt, especially when the conditions for hunting on foot are noisy.

A canoe is often the most practical way to transport the carcass back to camp.

noisy conditions by walking on logs, exposed tree roots, and pine needles.

One way for still-hunters to overcome noisy situations completely, turning them to their advantage, is heading for water. Shallow creeks, marshy areas, and rivers are perfect avenues to use to outwit whitetails and mule deer. Rubber boots are necessary for walking creeks or wet areas with water less than a foot deep. Hip boots or chest waders are a must for anything deeper. The hip waders are less cumbersome and noisy than the chest type.

A canoe offers the ultimate means for still-hunting rivers and streams. Gliding with the current in one of these streamlined crafts is much quieter than walking in water. Two men are best for still-hunting from a canoe: one steers and paddles and the other sits in the bow with rifle ready. It is often possible to float within close range of bedded or feeding deer while in a canoe.

Hunting on horseback is another form of still-hunting. Horse travel in deer country is most common in the West for muleys. Horses aren't as quiet as canoes, but deer don't seem to mind. Approaching them to within rifle range on horseback is possible. In the absence of conversation among riders, mule deer may view horses as elk.

One time when my brother Bruce and I were hunting mule deer in the Colorado Rockies with guide and outfitter Rudy Rudibaugh from Parlin, we rode up on a herd of deer that would have otherwise been difficult to approach. We were riding through willow brush above timberline when the group of five muleys, three of them bucks, got up

Stalkers often use spotting scopes to locate deer from high vantage points.

These deer hunters are glassing for bucks while their horses are grazing. Horses provide yet another means of still-hunting.

from their beds about 150 yards away. They stood and watched us, seemingly more curious than alarmed.

Bruce dismounted and grabbed his rifle from its scabbard. Not wanting to take an offhand shot, my brother started crawling toward a pile of rocks where he could steady the rifle. As he did, the deer got nervous and started to move off. Bruce quickly got into a sitting position and tried two shots, but both missed their mark—a buck with four points on one side and three on the other. Bruce was forced to shoot too quickly. If a rest had been handy where he dismounted, that buck would have been his.

Horses are most useful in stop-and-go hunting mountainous terrain as a means of transportation from one observation point to another. A common and productive practice for locating mule deer is stopping at high points overlooking basins or valleys. Binoculars or spotting scopes are then used to scan the visible terrain for deer. Glassing properly can take several hours at each stop. Bedded animals are often difficult to spot, but they usually get up at regular intervals to feed and can be detected then. Sometimes a deer will appear suddenly in a location where nothing was visible minutes before.

Once an animal a hunter wants to try for is spotted, a stalk is made. The cardinal rule for stalking in hilly terrain is always to approach from above. Deer seldom expect danger from above; consequently they spend most of their time looking downhill. If a deer is spotted above you while glassing or still-hunting, you should continue out of sight and hearing of the animal and climb above it before beginning a stalk.

Wind direction, hunter movement, and noise are just as important in stalking as in still-hunting. Any one of them can make or break the endeavor. The stalking hunter has an advantage over the still-hunter, however, because he has his quarry located. His major task is choosing the best course to take that will put him in range of a deer without giving himself away.

Always go into or across the wind to stalk a deer. If there is much wind, its direction can be determined easily. When it is light to gusty try dropping sand, snow, or light blades of grass to see which way they drift. The cool side of a wetted finger is also a clue to wind direction. A piece of thread tied to a bow or firearm and smoke from a lighted cigarette will aid hunters in determining air flow, too. When temperatures are below freezing, or close to it, a determination of air current direction can be made by exhaling and watching the vapor.

Even when great pains have been taken to stalk with the breeze in a hunter's favor the effort can be ruined by a change in wind direction, an unexplained gust, or a new current.

Try to be mindful of any change in wind patterns while stalking and, if necessary, make a change in course. If the only avenue of approach to a deer puts the hunter upwind of the animal, don't go after it if using a bow, shotgun, handgun, or musket. Hunters using high-powered rifles might be able to get within range before they are winded. If there is a possibility the animal will move to a more favorable position for a stalk or if the wind might change, it is best to wait.

If the breeze or air current is flowing downhill when above a buck, move down to the animal's elevation or slightly above, off to either side. When at an appropriate level stalk across the slope at a downhill angle or on a line with him.

Hunter movement isn't a problem in stalking if done under cover or at the right time. Try to plan a stalk to take advantage of such features of the terrain as gullies, river beds, valleys, hills, trees, brush, and rocks—and always consider the deer's behavior. Let's look at deer behavior first.

Any deer is easier to move in on when it is lying down rather than feeding. When on their feet, whitetails and mule deer are more alert than when bedded. Don't get me wrong, deer don't throw caution to the wind when they lie down, but they are more relaxed and less likely to detect a stalking hunter. An additional consideration for long stalks is that once bedded, deer usually remain in one place for at least an

This still-hunting archer caught deer in foreground by surprise.

hour. A feeding deer can move surprisingly far during a long stalk, which increases the chances of losing track of it or spooking it.

In many situations it may be difficult or impossible to wait for a deer to bed down before trying a stalk. If time isn't a problem and a deer can be kept in sight without alarming it, try to wait until a deer beds before attempting a stalk.

If stalking a deer that is feeding where cover is sparse, try to restrict movements to the intervals when the animal's head is down. Keeping a low profile by crawling on hands and knees or belly is advisable in such a situation. Deer will raise their heads at regular intervals to look around between bites. Be sure you are motionless when a buck or doe looks up.

Still-hunting proved to be the right technique for this young hunter to score.

When moving in on a feeding deer in a crouched or upright position it is best to shuffle your feet if you are on grass or other ground cover that isn't noisy. It is possible to be caught off balance, standing on one leg, when lifting feet to close the distance on a deer.

The sun can be an advantage to a stalking hunter if he approaches a deer with the sun at his back. If it is at the right angle, the strong backlighting can impair a deer's ability to spot a hunter. The same principle can be applied while still-hunting. Wind direction should be considered before sun angle, however, whether you are still-hunting or stalking.

Hunter movement isn't as important when stalking a deer from above as it is in other situations. Countless times members of my party and I have stalked deer from above in plain sight. If the animals had looked up they would have seen us, but few of them do. The advantages of moving in on deer from above can't be overemphasized.

Whenever possible plan a stalk so you will be out of a deer's sight throughout an approach. The best way to close the distance unseen is by heading down a valley or gulley or by aligning trees, brush, or rocks between you and the deer. If the screening cover isn't high enough to walk upright, crouch or crawl. Before starting out on such a stalk be sure to pick out landmarks to use as reference points; so you will know where to come out of a valley and where the deer is supposed to be. Prominent trees, fences, ridge lines, or rocks should be noted carefully.

It may be possible to check on a deer periodically during a stalk. If not, be doubly sure you know where you are going or work out a system of hand signals with a partner who will be able to see the deer. Also, make sure he knows when you will want directions.

When I want directions in such a situation, I wave my hat. When my partner holds both arms up, it means the deer is still there. Just the right or left arm extended means the deer moved that way. A wave back is a sign that the animal spooked. Additional signals can be added to expand communication between a stalker and lookout. Just be sure you both understand what they are before starting out on a stalk.

Noise can be kept to a minimum in stalking by taking advantage of the same guidelines listed for still-hunting. Noise isn't usually critical until within 100 yards or less of a deer, depending on ground and weather conditions. Beyond that point, stalkers can move in as quickly as possible without much regard for disturbance from sounds they make.

7

Drives

At certain times and in certain types of cover neither stand nor still-hunting is productive. Deer that don't move from their daytime resting areas until dark make sitting at a stand all day a waste of time. The same holds for a still-hunter: many of the deer in his area are too wary to get a shot at because they hole up in cover so thick that approaching them undetected is impossible.

When the two techniques are combined in a team effort, however, the chances of success improve and a third popular deer hunting method evolves: the drive.

Some groups of hunters rely almost exclusively on this technique all season. Their success usually explains why. The first whitetails my brother and I claimed were taken on drives. I was a stander when I dropped mine. Bruce's was collected as a driver. Both standers and drivers have a chance to connect on drives, but the odds usually favor hunters waiting on post.

There were five of us the day my brother and I scored. Besides ourselves there was an uncle, Leonard Yelle, his son Randy, and Jim Rankin, Leonard's brother-in-law. Our group size was just right for small drives. Leonard put Bruce and me on stands between 50 and 75 yards apart and instructed us to stay put until the drive was over. Jim also posted. Leonard and Randy made the push toward us.

It wasn't long before I heard something running toward me. A deer broke from cover moving from right to left about 30 yards away. It was

The first deer the author ever shot was taken on a drive (sketch credit: Sue LaFaive).

a doe, but I had an antlerless permit. I shouldered my 12-gauge pump and fired. I was using slugs.

The deer showed no immediate sign of a hit, continuing at a fast clip without faltering. I assumed I missed, but before she went out of sight, she fell. I found out later my slug hit the deer in the heart. My excitement knew no bounds that day. I became a deer hunter.

On the next drive our group switched assignments. Randy and Leonard were standers; Bruce, Jim, and I moved through a piece of cover toward them. Moments into the drive there was a shot, and Bruce had his deer. The whitetail almost ran him down in an effort to get away from Jim. It tried to escape by going to the side rather than straight ahead.

Drives can be broken down into three categories: quiet, noisy, and dog pack. The intent of all three is the same: to push deer from areas where they are resting or feeding, which are usually locations where their vulnerability to hunters is minimal, to standers. This is the only way hunters get a crack at some whitetail and mule deer.

Bucks that make it past the first few days of the hunting season often seek out the thickest patch of cover in their home range and stay there all day every day until the season is over. Travel is done at night, unless they are forced to do otherwise. Some deer follow these habits year-round, due to their age or the habitat they live in. For these reasons drives can be productive any time during deer season if they are organized and carried out properly.

Only two hunters are necessary to make a drive, but a group numbering from five to ten is much better. Upwards of 20 or more hunters can be too many for an effective drive, except when dogs are used. Some states limit the number of hunters who may take part in drives. The time required to organize a drive as well as the chances for a foulup increases proportionately with the number of participants, and this reduces hunting time.

To work effectively as a unit, drivers and standers should know the area being hunted. When new hunters are involved an explanation of the lay of the land by way of a map will help. An attribute at least as important as familiarity with an area is that participants be able to follow directions. Worthy of equal attention is that there be someone to give directions and assign duties: a hunt captain or leader.

The only difference between a quiet and noisy drive, as the names

Drives take a lot of planning. Here a pair of drivers map their strategy.

imply, is the amount of disturbance made by drivers. On a noisy drive, for example, drivers sometimes blow whistles, beat on pans, shout, bark like dogs, and break branches in an effort to scare deer from hiding places and make them run to standers waiting ahead. On a quiet drive, drivers move toward standers without making an unusual amount of noise. They may advance as if they were still-hunting or as if going for a casual stroll, but not trying to conceal their presence.

Quiet drives are usually more effective than loud drives. The noise made by drivers often has an effect opposite from its intent. Instead of scaring deer into panicking and running blindly toward standers, the animals often stay put, go out the ends, or between the drivers. This is especially true of the wise bucks who have survived one or two drives. Deer are simply tipped off to the positions of drivers by the noise they make, and the animals use the information to their advantage.

One season I hunted from a stand that was in a narrow section of woods. That piece of cover proved to be a favored area for drives by a group of hunters I didn't know. It was obvious a drive was in progress when a line of men moved toward me shouting and barking like dogs.

I stayed put, hoping they would push a buck by me. They didn't. More to the point, however, was the fact none of the drivers saw me, and they made the push three days in a row. I was wearing red and not as concealed as a deer would have been. Any deer in the area could have escaped detection as I did—by staying put. Most of them probably did.

The first two days the drive was conducted there were no shots fired. I did see one deer, a fawn, that was a direct result of the drive. It came from the direction the drivers were moving after they passed by! The youngster didn't want to go the way they wanted him to and slipped through the line.

On the third day the drivers pushed the cover there were shots fired, apparently by a stander. From the shouting that followed I assume a deer was bagged; so noisy drives do work once in a while.

The primary function of drivers—jumping and moving deer ahead of them—can be accomplished with more consistency on a quiet drive. Any deer in the drivers' paths will hear them occasionally as a twig is snapped or leaves rustled, but usually not enough to determine where they are at all times. This uncertainty is apt to make the deer nervous and move out.

Some deer may still hold tight or slip through the line, but the chances of it happening are reduced. Drivers on a quiet push should be looking closely for deer as they go. They may spot one bedded or sneaking away from another driver. Noisy drives reduce the chances that drivers will get to shoot. I'm sure my brother's tag would have gone unfilled that year we both scored on successive drives if we would have tried to push the deer by intentionally making noise.

Noisy drives do have advantages, according to some advocates of the practice. Standers can keep track of the progress of the drive and each driver, eliminating the chances of a shot fired in their direction. Each driver also knows where his partners are and can maintain the desired formation or spacing while moving ahead. But there are ways to accomplish the same ends by different means on quiet drives.

First of all, it isn't critical that standers be able to follow the progress of the drivers. Posted hunters should be alert from the time they get into position until the push is completed. On a quiet drive, drivers can signal standers if and when deer are jumped by shouting, "Here they come," or "Heads up," to make sure standers will be ready. Another signal I've used is firing a .22 rimfire handgun when I jump deer on a drive. Such a signal also alerts other drivers to be on their toes. Once the deer are moving, sound made by the driver that jumped them won't make much difference.

As far as drivers keeping tabs on one another, they should be close enough to see each other at intervals on the most effective pushes. When this isn't possible, they can whistle, hoot, or caw once in a while to maintain contact. Well-spaced whistles, owl hoots, or crow caws may be accepted as natural sounds by deer and not associated with hunters. On the other hand, they may not be. It is best for drivers not to make any sounds at all if possible. Drivers familiar with an area and their partners' paces should be able to progress properly without aural assistance.

More often than not, driven deer are far enough ahead of drivers so any shots fired by standers won't endanger them. To be on the safe side, however, drivers can move to the sides as they approach standers on the chance a deer may not show himself until the last possible moment. An alternative is for drivers to announce themselves by whistling or calling as they near standers. Drivers must be familiar with the driven area to use either technique.

Neither of these precautions should be necessary in my opinion. It goes without saying that drivers and standers alike should never take a shot in a direction that might endanger a partner. And above all else, hunters should be sure of their target before shooting regardless of the hunting technique used, but especially on drives where hunters can be in close proximity to one another.

No whitetail or mule deer, no matter how big, is worth wounding or killing a fellow hunter for. If it is considered unsafe for both drivers and standers to carry firearms or bows, drivers should leave their weapons behind until taking their turn at posting. The usual procedure is for drivers and standers to alternate duties. Hunters who have filled their tag join the ranks of the drivers for the rest of the season in our group. The fellow who quits hunting after bagging his deer is seldom invited along again, unless there is a good reason for dropping out of the hunt.

Terrain that you and hunting partners are most familiar with is the best to drive for deer. It is important to know where deer bed, feed, and travel in order to plan a drive effectively. This information should be readily available about your home territory.

The smaller the area that can be isolated for a drive, the better. A swamp, valley, ravine, thicket, or wood lot that is a quarter mile or less on a side is ideal. Cover that is narrower than it is long is best of all for a drive.

Areas larger than a quarter mile can and are driven successfully, but the deer's chances of escaping increases as the size of the area increases. More area means more cover for deer to hide in unnoticed and wider gaps in the line of drivers for deer to slip through. A quarter mile is simply a guideline, not a hard and fast rule. I have had my best success on drives conducted in areas within that size range. Another general rule is drives work well in the thickest cover around.

Any number of natural and manmade features can be used to isolate a driveable tract of land. Roads, rivers, lakes, ridges, power lines, railroad tracks, and such changes in cover as where swamps change to hardwoods, hardwoods to fields, timber to meadows, and sagebrush to aspens are examples of convenient borders. Cover that is very long, but narrow, might best be driven in stages.

If you can't think of suitable areas to drive in terrain you frequent or if you want to discover new possibilities, checking out a map or aerial photographs are good ways to locate suitable spots. Topographical or quadrangle maps are best for this purpose. All features of the terrain are clearly marked.

Once a location or two has been decided on for drives, picking stands is the next step. This is where the chances of success for many drives disappears. The idea is not to choose stands where you want the deer to go, but where they want to go when jumped. Deer can seldom be forced to go where they don't want to. Few drives succeed in doing so. Hunters should use their knowledge of normal deer behavior and use of escape routes to determine where to place standers.

In the morning, deer generally move from feeding grounds to bedding areas. Many of them may already be bedded by daylight, especially after they have been hunted for several days. The trend reverses in the evening—deer move from bedding to feeding grounds. Deer will be bedded during a large part of the day.

Generally, drives should be made from feeding toward bedding areas in the early morning. Pushes at other periods will be through bedding grounds themselves. Bedded deer are the focal point of most drives I've been on.

For morning drives, if bedding and feeding areas are not far apart, say from a quarter to half a mile, standers should be positioned far enough beyond bedding locations (100 to 200 yards) so they won't spook any deer that are there when getting in position. When close to a mile separates the two key locations, the area can be driven in stages.

Deer jumped on a drive in the evening will not head toward feeding grounds as they normally would, unless that direction offers the most security. Their first reaction is to get away from what disturbed them. Bedding areas are often in thick cover; consequently, they mean safety to deer. A deer's dinner table, on the other hand, is often in open country, which whitetails and mule deer try to avoid during daylight hours when being hunted. This explains why deer will go toward bedding areas on morning drives but aren't likely to head for chow when driven in the latter part of the day.

Outside of early morning drives then, standers should be located along escape routes. These routes normally lead from bedding areas toward the nearest patch of cover where deer hope to elude hunters. Escape routes may follow valleys, narrow necks of woods, or go over ridges.

If you have jumped deer from bedding areas before, you should have an idea which way they are likely to go. If not, do your best to calculate routes moved deer are apt to take. Take the wind into consideration when doing so. Deer always try to move with the breeze in their face so they can smell what is ahead. Sometimes they travel crosswind for a distance, too. If they are jumped going with the wind, they won't often go far in that direction. Due to variable wind conditions from day to day, deer may use different escape routes to best take advantage of their sense of smell.

Standers can avoid, or at least reduce the chances, of being winded by positioning themselves so their scent isn't blowing directly toward where deer are expected to appear. Elevated stands, where legal, are a great help in this respect.

Some of the best stands may be to either side of the line of drivers or, believe it or not, behind them rather than directly in front. Remember, deer go where they want to on a drive, not where the hunters want

94

them to. Standers who connect will be covering locations where jumped deer normally travel when alarmed.

In the event deer were jumped and not seen by standers, an effort should be made to find out why. A lesson can be learned by failure of a drive if hunters are willing to take the time to do it. Most don't. An escape route a buck used successfully once will be used again if he is in the same area.

Snow makes the job of unraveling how deer made their getaway easier, but telltale signs can often be found under other conditions as well. It is at least worth a try. If their escape route is discovered, be sure to have a hunter watching it the next time that area is driven. It may pay off.

Snow on the ground gives hunters a slight edge when making a drive. Any deer in the area, whether feeding or bedded, will have left tracks, unless the snow fell recently. One driver should be assigned to follow the tracks with the others to either side of him. Men to the sides should try to adjust their courses according to the tracker's progress.

The best way to accomplish this is to have the tracker whistle, bark periodically or carry a bell so others can keep track of him. This is a variation of a noisy drive that can be very productive. Once the deer is jumped the odds of someone getting a shot are good, whether it is standers or the drivers to the sides.

Standers should be as quiet as possible when going to their posts, as well as once there. Too much noise can alert deer to their presence and whitetail or muleys will steer clear of them just as easily as they do of noisy drivers. If standers aren't cautious, they could spook deer out of an area before a drive begins.

The chances of running into a deer on the way to a stand shouldn't be discounted, unless it is dark. I bagged my first buck on the way to a stand preceding a drive. Deer may just as easily travel by standers on their own before a drive begins, too; so standers should always be alert.

Try to have standers in as many strategic positions as possible. Assigning them all to positions facing the drivers just because "that's the way a normal drive operates" is a mistake. If there are enough hunters, put some on the sides and behind the drivers. When a drive is made into the wind, bucks sometimes circle back through the line of drivers and think they are home free.

On drives made with the wind at the drivers' backs most of the standers should be to the sides and behind unless the drivers are so close together deer aren't likely to get through. If deer are able to smell

This buck was taken by a stander on the way to his stand, before drive began. Standers should always be alert for deer.

drivers, it has the same effect as a noisy affair. The animals are able to tell where the hunters are and will either stay put or circle back if they can.

The rear and sides can sometimes be covered best by still-hunters. Hunters on either side of the heavy cover should move with the drivers or slightly ahead of them. Tail-end hunters should follow from 50 to 100 yards behind the drivers.

More often than not, drivers are started at prearranged times. Standers are given from 15 minutes to a half hour or more to get in position; then the drivers start in. All watches should be synchronized for this purpose. Sometimes a car horn or whistle is used to signal both the beginning and end of a drive.

Instead of sitting in a vehicle or relaxing while waiting for standers to get in position, drivers should be standing on the edge of cover or just inside it until time to go unless, of course, it is dark. If standers do move deer on their way in, drivers may get shooting before starting out. I recall one time I should have done just that instead of passing the time in the car.

There were four of us that day. I was going to be the only driver because there was snow and the wind was right. Tracks would be easy to follow and I could get any deer moving that were in the piece of cover we planned on pushing.

Just after I started in I found a lone, fresh track coming out. It was big, and I felt sure a buck made it. Those tracks were made by a deer my partners jumped when they reached their stands. The story was clear by the time I reached them. If I had been where I should have been I might have claimed an easy buck.

The standers didn't see any deer on that drive, of course. The animals had been alerted and moved out before I started in. This example points out the importance of standers being as quiet as possible on their way to stands.

An important rule of drives is that standers stay put until the push is over. They should wait until hearing a prearranged signal or someone picks them up. If any deer are taken, everyone normally lends a hand getting them out of the woods. Following up a deer that is hit and runs off or dressing an animal should be postponed until the hunt is over. The same goes when drivers connect. They should mark the kill and go back for it later with other members of the group.

Use of dogs to drive deer is a tactic only practiced on whitetails in North America and in limited areas. Hounds are not permitted to chase mule deer during the course of a hunt.

The only states where driving with hounds is now legal are in the southeastern U.S. Deer hunting with dogs used to be practiced in northern parts of the country, but was outlawed there about 1900. In areas of the South where dogs are still permitted to hunt deer, the cover is so thick that canines are the best means of moving whitetails out of swamps to where hunters can get shots at them. Human drivers would pass by most deer without getting them moving in that terrain. Hounds can sniff the deer out.

Canada's Province of Ontario also permits the use of dogs to drive deer.

A hunt with hounds is started by finding a fresh track crossing a road or by casting hounds into an area where they are expected to jump a deer. Either way, standers are positioned strategically in the location to be hunted before the chase begins. Standers are often positioned in a horseshoe or S-shaped pattern.

Some members of the party usually try to stay with the dogs and serve as drivers, too. They help get deer moving and steer dogs toward posted hunters when starting out looking for a fresh trail. Once a chase is over the drivers also catch the dogs.

Since a pack of dogs, usually numbering from three to six (some hunters use only one), often stays on the trail of one deer for some time, a chase may be stopped if they are on a doe. Some deer dogs reportedly prefer the track of a buck. Deer are easily able to stay ahead of dogs on such hunts. They are normally sneaking or trotting along 300 to 500 yards ahead of their pursuers rather than running flat out directly

Hounds are commonly used to drive deer in parts of the southeastern United States and the province of Ontario in Canada.

in front of them. The commotion created by driving dogs also moves deer that aren't being chased. For these reasons, standers must be constantly alert. A flicker of movement is often the only hint of an approaching whitetail.

Beagles and basset hounds are preferred by some hunters because they move whitetails at a leisurely pace and watchers have more of a chance at a standing or slowly moving target. Others prefer bigger black-and-tans, Walkers or July hounds to keep deer moving at a steady pace. Purebred dogs are by no means the only types used for deer hunting. Mongrels are found in many packs. Dogs that only run the freshest track are preferred to those that try to follow a trail that is hours old.

Dog hunting for deer requires as much coordination and planning, if not more so, as other types of drives. Hounds are not only useful to push deer to standers, but they also follow up and find wounded whitetails that might otherwise be lost.

Much of the dog hunting in the South is done by organized hunting clubs. The best advice for hunters who would like to try this type of hunting is to contact the department of natural resources in a state they want to hunt for a listing of hunting clubs. States that permit hunting deer with dogs include Louisiana, Georgia, North Carolina, Alabama, Florida, Mississippi, and Texas. In many of these states hunting with hounds is only permitted in specified areas, not statewide.

8

Tracking

The general principles involved in hunting whitetail and mule deer by tracking them are simple: find a track in the snow, preferably fresh, and follow it. Hunters who stay with a set of tracks long enough will get the deer that made them.

Perseverance, physical endurance, and stealth are three of the qualities hunters who want to track deer successfully should possess. They must also feel at ease wherever deer lead them, free from worry about getting lost. A hunter preoccupied with that fear will not be able to devote the concentration to the tracking technique necessary to make it work.

Use of tracking to bag deer is usually restricted to the northern and mountain states and provinces where snowfall is common during deer seasons. The method would probably prove to be impractical in sandy areas under most circumstances.

Despite the fact that tracking as a hunting technique is restricted to certain geographical areas, all deer hunters should try to develop the skill. There are times when, despite how well a deer is hit with gun or bow, the animal will travel out of sight before going down. For this reason, hunters should be proficient at tracking deer under all conditions.

The hunting form of tracking can be practiced successfully in most terrains and covers; however, the chances of scoring are greatest in country that is predominantly hardwood-covered hills or mountains with scattered pockets and stands of evergreens. The odds also favor the tracking hunter in open bog country and similar terrain.

Visibility is greatest in these situations, which increases the chances of the tracker spotting his quarry. The broken nature of hilly terrain makes it easier to move in on deer undetected. Another advantage common in this habitat is that deer densities are usually not high. This reduces the possibility of confusing the track of a deer being followed with that of other animals.

Fresh snow is ideal for this method of deer hunting, but not a necessity. Conditions that are best for tracking deer are after a heavy snowfall coats all trees and brush or in the fog. Sound doesn't travel far under these circumstances. Deer can't see far either. Wet or crusted snow is fair to poor for tracking.

There is an easy way to gauge how old deer tracks are in the morning regardless of the snow conditions present. A friend of mine, Duaine Wenzel, uses this system all the time. He usually gets up at least once during the night and makes a footprint in the snow or flips a board, brick, or piece of wood over. Before leaving to look for deer tracks in the morning Duaine checks a fresh boot print against the imprint made during the night and has a rough idea what a fresh deer track will look like as opposed to one several hours old.

If it snowed during the night Wenzel will be able to judge a deer track's age by the amount of snow in it. On warm nights a track's age

This tracking deer hunter checks out a set of prints under ideal tracking conditions.

will be determined by how much it has melted. Prints made during periods of cold will freeze and sometimes ice crystals will form in them, depending on their age. It is often necessary to feel a print to assess how frozen it is.

Before going any further let's discuss what deer tracks look like. Whitetail and mule deer hooves are made up of two segments. There is a noticeable gap between the halves that widens near their tips. Each half is narrower at the front than at the rear, often almost pointed. The back end of each "toe" is more rounded than the front. A pair of dew claws are a short distance above the rear of each foot on the back of the leg.

When walking on solid ground in snow that isn't more than an inch deep, dew claws seldom show. Each print looks something like a pair of elongated drops of moisture side by side. Dew claws are usually visible when a deer walks on soft ground, in snow several inches deep, or when he runs. They appear as a pair of small depressions or marks behind or at the base of each "droplet."

Bounding deer bunch their feet together. Prints from the hind feet will be imprinted forward of the front feet. Tracks of a walking deer will be almost in a straight line with the left and right footprints staggered either side of center.

Closeup of a deer's hoof with dew claws shown.

Deer tracks look like this. Each of two toes are pointed in front and rounded at the rear.

Duaine, like most tracking hunters, prefers to go after bucks, the biggest he can find. So he simply looks for the biggest, freshest track around. A few roads are checked by car, first, before daylight. If he doesn't find a good track that way, he zig-zags through the woods until finding one. He usually knows what territory several good bucks occupy through preseason scouting. When searching out big bucks in hilly or mountainous terrain the best procedure is to go up—unless heavy snows have pushed them off the summits to lower elevations.

There are ways to distinguish a buck's track from that of a doe. I know a pair of brothers, Jerry and Terry Weigold, who do it consistently. The problem is explaining the differences to another hunter. They weren't able to explain how they do it to me. Through experience they just know a buck track when they see one.

Duaine Wenzel is the same way. He told me, "There is a pace they make that I know is a buck. It takes experience to recognize it."

Generally, a buck is more likely to leave drag marks from his feet in the snow than a doe. Generally, bucks' prints point slightly outward rather than straight ahead like doe tracks. Generally, bucks will leave bigger tracks than does. Generally, two or three sets of tracks together, one adult and the others small, will be a doe and her young of the year.

The best advice I can come up with for choosing a track to follow that is likely to be a buck is to do as Wenzel does - pick the biggest track possible. After following it a mile you should know for sure if you

Tracking hunter checks bed of doe a buck he was trailing led him to. A deer that frequently leads the tracker to other deer beds is usually a buck.

are on the track of a buck. By then they often rub their antlers on a sapling, scrape the ground and urinate in the area, or leave an imprint of the tips of their antlers in the snow while feeding. Sometimes only one or two tines will touch the snow when a buck lowers his head to pick up a morsel of food; so look closely for any telltale marks in the snow.

Tracks from a buck in the rut will frequently lead the tracker to beds vacated by does, as the animal looks for prospective mates. Another sign to look for are drops of urine that fall as the deer walks. Occasionally a courting whitetail or muley will get in a fight with another buck. The evidence of such a battle should be plain in the snow. If no positive indications of a deer's sex have been seen after covering a mile or more, it is best to stick with the trail unless a bigger print that is fresh has been seen.

If the track a hunter is following is one of the biggest in the area, there shouldn't be any problem confusing it with others. On the chance a print of similar size might be encountered, however, hunters should look for anything unusual about prints made by a deer they intend to pursue, to avoid possible confusion. One segment of a hoof may be shorter than the other, for instance, or the toes may be rounded more than normal.

Tracking hunters should adjust their pace to correspond with the deer's gait that they are following. If the animal is walking at a steady pace, the hunter should try to do the same. Hunters should move as fast as they can after a deer that is running. When a buck is poking along feeding, a following hunter should slow down to a crawl and be "careful as heck," as Wenzel says.

Whitetail and mule deer usually start to feed before they bed down. While feeding they often loop back and forth nipping at browse. Deer usually eat the tips of plants, bushes, and young trees. The ends will be ragged where the tips are broken off by browsing animals.

Try to go as straight as possible when following a feeding deer. Look as far ahead as possible in an effort to sort out the track visually to avoid making all of the loops the deer made. It may take as long as five minutes to sort out the trail with your eyes, but it is usually worth it. Bedded deer don't think a hunter coming straight at them is as dangerous as one who is making every swing they did. A zigzagging hunter is also more visible to a deer that is bedded.

When moving in on a whitetail or muley try to avoid making noise. Move branches and brush aside that may slap or rub against you or your weapon. It is best to detour around dense patches of cover that can't be negotiated quietly. Also try to avoid stepping on twigs that may snap.

All noises that might be made won't necessarily spook deer. The woods are full of noises. After making a sound that may alert an animal

A skillful tracker will catch sight of deer in this position. This one doesn't have antlers, but trackers who pick the largest track in their area stand a good chance of spotting a buck like this.

you are trailing, it sometimes helps to pause for several minutes before moving further ahead.

Hunters should keep alert for any sounds deer might make. When not alarmed whitetails and muleys sometimes make a lot of noise when feeding. They pull on brush and break twigs. It is even possible to hear them chew when they are close. The animals seldom feed continuously. They go "crunch, crunch, crunch"; then they pause for a look around. Hunters who hear a feeding deer ahead can move during the brief intervals the buck is noisy. When that close to a whitetail or muley, it is usually best to stay put and wait for the deer to make the moves. If you are patient enough, it should eventually step into view.

Deer sometimes give their positions away by making noises while they are walking. When a tracking hunter hears an animal ahead of him, however, it is more often running or bounding than walking. A walking deer might snap a twig or slosh through mud hard enough to make a thudding sound. Brush-breaking noises often accompany the hasty departure of whitetails and muleys, too.

A hunter's eyes are usually more important than his ears for detecting the presence of his quarry. Try to concentrate your attention on the area ahead at a 45-degree angle left and right. Don't spend much time looking far left and right until the cover ahead has been scanned carefully. Stoop down and look low, too. Visibility is often better from this angle. It sometimes helps to divide the terrain into sections and scan them individually.

Deer other than the one being trailed are commonly seen; so when you see an animal, don't assume it is the one you have been after. Try to get a good look at it before deciding to shoot. Duaine has taken bucks other than the ones he was tracking on two different occasions. My brother Bruce made a mistake one time while following a buck and shot a doe. He wasn't as careful as he normally would have been because his tag was valid for either sex.

Deer that are being trailed frequently go past other animals; then the deer stop and watch the animals reactions to tip them off at the approach of a hunter. Tracking hunters who spot deer other than the one they are following should try not to spook them. If they are allowed to go on their way unalarmed, the animal being followed will frequently drop its guard.

Another trick deer that are being tailed pull is to stop after climbing a hill or crossing a clearing to watch for their pursuer. Savvy hunters can often get the drop on a buck by circling a hill or clearing to come in from the rear or side.

The stealthier a hunter is, the sooner he will get a look and maybe a

Deer that are being trailed will often stop on a hill to wait for their pursuer. Trackers who are alert might be able to get the drop on a deer who tries this by circling ahead *(photo credit: Montana Dept. of Fish & Game).*

shot at his deer. Even without stealth a tracker who perseveres long enough will eventually get a chance at a buck being trailed. Whitetails and mule deer gradually come to accept the hunter and even get curious. They invariably make a mistake.

"If I could follow a deer four days, I could shoot it," Wenzel says.

Many times it is possible to score the first day a buck's track is picked up. Other times, it may take several days. Whitetail bucks have a tendency to return to their home area during the night after being trailed for miles; so their tracks can frequently be started in the same general area on successive days. Mule deer are less likely to do this. A big muley's track would probably have to be picked up where it was left the night before on successive days of tracking.

One time Wenzel jumped a whitetail buck from beds yards apart two days in a row. Duaine got several shots at the animal the first day when it jumped, but missed. He reloads his own rifle ammunition, but rather than take the time to pick up the brass, he hustled after the buck. He estimated he followed that animal eight miles that day without getting another crack at it.

The next morning he returned to the place where he shot at the buck to pick up his brass. Just short of the spot, the buck jumped up. Caught by surprise, Duaine didn't get a shot. He eventually bagged the deer that day though. As the whitetail stood up from its third bed, Wenzel nailed him.

Shots frequently have to be taken in a hurry when tracking deer. Wenzel prepares for the season by practicing throwing his rifle to his shoulder and getting on target. He uses a six-and-a-half-pound .30-06 with a 1-4X variable scope. He fires 180-grain round-nosed bullets.

Like most experienced hunters who regularly track deer, Duaine is familiar with the areas he hunts. When trailing a deer he usually knows where he is and what lies ahead. This information sometimes helps him anticipate the route a buck will take. Over the years he has noticed that different bucks in the same vicinity have a tendency to travel through the same localities when pushed.

The beginning tracking hunter can't expect to be as skillful as an old hand at the technique right away. It takes years to develop the familiarity with the lay of the land and the animals that live on it that Duaine and others like him have developed. Regardless of whether or not hunters who track deer connect, the experience is bound to be educational. Deer give their pursuers cram courses on what they eat, the habitat they prefer, their daily habits, and how clever they can be in staying out of sight. They don't give hunters lessons willingly, of course; those who want to learn must interpret buck signs left in the snow for hours and sometimes days.

All deer hunters, regardless of the hunting technique they use, should assume a whitetail or muley they shoot at is hit. Most animals will give some indication of being struck, but not always. Deer that stagger, hunch up, kick, leap in the air, favor a leg or break into a dead run after a shot are usually hit. Bowhunters can sometimes actually see their arrows strike deer.

If you know the deer you shot at is hit, that is usually good. A properly placed bullet or arrow will put a deer down in seconds, many times on the spot or within sight. It is the ones that are hit that make it out of sight before dropping that I will discuss here.

Try to make a mental note of where deer are standing when you shoot at them. This can be done after the animal has gone out of sight. Unless there is a good chance for another shot at a deer, it is best to stay where you shot from rather than immediately racing after a whitetail or muley. If it is hit seriously, it may lie down just out of sight. A hunter who stumbles after a wounded animal right away sometimes reduces his chances of getting it.

Always try to watch a deer that has been shot at as long as possible. If it didn't show any signs of being hit at first, it may while in flight.

When shooting at a deer, watch for any reaction that might mean a hit. This buck hunched up when hit.

Noting the course the animal follows will also make locating its trail easier.

Keep your ears open, too. A fleeing deer that is out of sight but within earshot makes a lot of noise. If the animal falls, you should be able to tell it and get a fix on the approximate location.

Once a deer that may be wounded is out of sight and hearing and you have the spot or spots marked where it was when you shot, walk directly there. It is a good idea to leave a hat or coat to mark the spot where the shot was taken from, unless there is a prominent identifying feature nearby. Bowhunters should look for their arrow if unsure of a hit. Gun hunters should look for blood, hair, or anything between where they shot from and where the deer stood to determine if their bullet may have hit.

Archers who find a bloodied arrow know they scored a hit. If the search turns up a clean broadhead, the shot was a miss. A missing shaft might also mean the arrow was on target. Look for blood or hair if the arrow can't be found.

Tufts of hair or blood are sure signs of a hit for hunters. Look for these clues behind where the deer was standing as well as at the spot. Firearms users who find a tree their slug hit before reaching a deer can almost count on a miss. It is worthwhile to check further before giving up in such a situation.

Bowhunters who find a bloodied arrow know they scored a hit.

Tracking wounded deer in the snow is often easy. This archer inspects spot of blood left by deer he hit.

Location of a hit can often be determined by the color of hair or blood. Dark brown hair usually means the animal was struck in the chest or upper body. It will be light brown if the deer was hit in the shoulder. White hair originates from legs and the belly area.

Pink, frothy blood means a dead deer—it was hit in the lungs. Dark, beet-colored blood indicates a liver wound. Bright red blood usually comes from an artery. Watery blood or none at all and food particles or intestinal matter are evidence of a hit in the stomach or intestines.

If unable to determine if a deer was hit by checking the area where it was standing, move along the course it took after the shot, but try to make as little disturbance as possible. Look for blood on the ground or bushes. Archers can also keep an eye open for a broken arrow lying off to the side. There shouldn't be any problem following a deer in snow or sand. In blankets of leaves or pine needles look for areas where leaves and turf have been kicked up by a running deer. Vegetation will be flattened and broken in fields and openings where a deer went through. Hunters who carefully watched the departure of deer they shot at should not have trouble following the animal's trail for 100 yards or more. There should be some sign of a hit uncovered in that distance, but go as far as possible to be absolutely sure.

If it can be determined that a deer was hit in the lungs, there is no need to wait before following it. Enough blood should be present to easily follow the animal's trail the short distance it traveled. If it is raining or snowing there will be little choice but to follow up on a deer as soon as possible.

With a hit anywhere but in the shoulder area, it is best to wait before trying to trail a wounded deer. Don't worry if it is getting dark. As long as the weather stays clear you can go back and trail with a flashlight or lantern. Drops of blood often show up well under the illumination of a lantern.

When unsure of how badly a deer is wounded, waiting 30 minutes to an hour is usually long enough before picking up the trail. Try to hold off longer on paunch-shot animals. Five minutes can seem like a long time when you are anxious to follow a wounded deer; so it is best to try to do something to keep yourself occupied while waiting. If hunting with a partner or two it is a good idea to go get them to help trail. It will

Some states allow the use of dogs on leash to track wounded deer. Here a German Wire-Haired Pointer is being used to track a deer.

make the job easier. If alone, a walk to your car or camp is a good way to waste some time.

Hunters who have access to a dog that will track deer should consider getting it. Many states have laws prohibiting the use of dogs to trail deer; however, exceptions are often made in cases of wounded animals if a dog is restrained on a leash. Be sure to get an okay from a local game warden or department of natural resources official if unsure of the regulation pertaining to dogs.

Before leaving the spot where the deer was hit be sure you will be able to find it again. Leave a bright-colored hat or garment there or use ribbon to mark a course to the nearest road if the area will be difficult to relocate.

Try to start trailing a wounded deer from the point where it was last seen. If there is a moderate to heavy blood trail or snow, there shouldn't be any problem following the animal. Skill and painstaking care are necessary to unravel a trail with little or no blood. This is where a tracking dog can be a big advantage.

Lacking a dog, scour every inch of the ground for the tiniest drops of blood and tracks left by a wounded deer. It is sometimes necessary to get down on hands and knees when searching for minute details. Wounded whitetails and muleys run more often than not; so the ground should be noticeably disturbed along the route taken.

Be sure to look at bushes and tree trunks that the deer may have brushed past. Blood will often show in these locations.

It is advisable to mark every spot where a drop of blood or track from a wounded deer is found. Plastic surveyor's tape is perfect for this purpose. White ribbon, pieces of string, or tissue will also work. Place markers on bushes or tree limbs where they can be easily seen. After several markers have been hung it is usually possible to get a general idea of the animal's direction of travel by looking back.

Try to circle ahead and to the sides when the trail is lost. It isn't unusual for deer to make abrupt changes in direction. Be alert for any deviations. If the trail is lost entirely, keep in mind that whitetails and muleys, if seriously hurt, follow a path of least resistance. They tend to go downhill rather than uphill, for instance. Additionally, wounded deer may head for nearby heavy cover or water.

Exhaust every effort possible to locate a wounded deer. Perseverance often pays off in this type of tracking as it does when using the technique to hunt. If the animal isn't located, it probably wasn't seriously injured. While tracking a wounded deer, be ready to shoot again on the chance the animal isn't dead.

Deer hunters who are proficient with gun or bow and are

Flagging is good for marking where spots of blood are found when trailing a deer on bare ground.

conscientious about only taking the best shot possible can avoid unnecessary wounding. Because of variables involved in deer hunting, many of which hunters don't have control over, some wounding does occur. Few of these animals will go unrecovered if hunters follow the guidelines listed above for tracking them.

9

Calling Deer

At certain times it is actually possible to attract deer to a hunter rather than having to go to them or waiting where they might pass by. The techniques take advantage of the animals' mating instincts, curiosity, and in the case of whitetails, their territoriality.

There are two ways to bring deer to you. The most consistently productive is rattling a set of antlers together to simulate a fight between two bucks. Mouth-blown calls also bring deer in if the circumstances are right. Most deer calls are designed to sound like the bleat of a doe or a fawn in trouble.

The practice of rattling antlers to attract bucks originated in Texas and is commonly accepted there. It has been proven productive in other states, too, but isn't widely used. The method merits more use in many areas. In Michigan, for example, rattling for bucks is just about unheard of, but it works there.

An Upper Peninsula resident, Dave Paquette, tried it for the first time last fall and got a ten-point buck for his efforts. Five to ten minutes from the time Dave started twisting tines together the whitetail came trotting into view. It was opening day of the state's November firearms season. He had practiced rattling on three occasions during the week before the season and brought another buck in on his last attempt.

Rattling is most effective during the rut, which usually starts in late October or early November in northern states and December or January in the South. There may be other variations in timing of the rut

Rattling antlers simulates a pair of bucks fighting like these two. They do more pushing and shoving than smashing headlong into each other *(photo credit: Bob Landis)*.

from state to state. Deer in Florida, for instance, seem to breed at all times of the year with no peak breeding period.

The onset of cool weather in the fall usually triggers the rut, which can last for a month or more. Fights between bucks normally start over a doe that is ready to breed or when a buck catches a competing male in his territory. A third buck will investigate a fight out of curiosity—to join in if the squabble is in his stomping grounds or in an attempt to make off with the doe the fight might be over.

Mule deer don't establish territories like whitetails; so they aren't as responsive to rattled antlers. The technique still works on them, however. A muley buck drawn to the sounds of a battle between two other bucks would be interested in any does that might be around or just curious.

The chances of rattling working in areas where there are a lot of does and few bucks aren't good. The same is true of locations where hunter densities are high. Under this circumstance the odds favor attracting other hunters rather than deer. Large numbers of hunters are seldom a problem during archery deer seasons. Bow seasons would be the best time to try rattling in many states as long as they coincide with the rut.

Either whitetail or mule deer antlers will bring in bucks when rattled. The fresher they are the better, but an old set will do if that is all that is available. Check with a taxidermist or a friend who has plenty of antlers if you don't have any of your own. Generally, big racks are better than small ones, and the antlers should be as evenly matched as possible. Small, unmatched beams will work though.

To remove antlers from a skull, saw them off either below or above the burr. Also remove the brow tine and sharp tips of additional tines. A file can be used to smooth any ragged or rough areas. A carrying strap can be rigged for the antlers by drilling a hole through each base, putting a piece of leather or rope through them, then tying a knot in the ends of the material.

You might consider painting the antlers red or orange to be on the safe side, so there will be little chance of another hunter mistaking your rattling for the real thing.

Early in the morning on a cool, quiet day is the best time to rattle. Any time of the day can be productive, however. Bucks are jittery on windy days, and the sound of antlers rubbed together doesn't travel far then.

The best place to try the technique is near a series of scrapes. The buck that made them isn't likely to be far away and won't take kindly to what he thinks are a pair of other bucks having it out on his doorstep.

Always try to approach a rattling location quietly. Don't slam car doors or talk if you are with another hunter. It is a good idea for two hunters to work as a team when trying to rattle in a buck. One should plan on doing the shooting and the other the rattling. The guy with the antlers should be as concealed as possible in a position next to a tree or in brush.

Also try to select a calling site where an approaching buck will have some cover. They don't like to cross openings. Their tendency to avoid openings can be used to your advantage if a stand is chosen with a clearing downwind. Bucks coming to a fight will sometimes circle downwind. If there is an opening there, those that circle will have to expose themselves before they can wind you.

When two bucks fight they do more twisting and shoving than beating their antlers together. Keep this in mind when trying to imitate a battle. Bang the antlers together as loud as possible at first, then twist and turn them so the tines knock against each other and make as much noise as possible. Additional realistic sound effects can be made by pounding the bases of the antlers on the ground and raking them up and down a tree trunk or through brush. If gravel or rocks are common in your area scrape an antler through or over them. The object is to make noise; so don't be timid about it.

116

The procedure can be varied any way you like. Simply try to make the sounds realistic. It is a good idea to practice with the antlers at home to get a feel for how they should be manipulated.

Make as few movements as possible during the process of rattling antlers. If a buck shows and sees you instead of what he is expecting, he won't hang around long. You will never know he was there if he sees you before you see him.

Antlers should be rattled for as long as a couple of minutes; then take a break from three to five minutes to look around. A buck may come charging in or he may sneak. Try to be prepared for either. Curious deer will sometimes stop on the edge of cover; so look closely.

After a pause, go through the motions again of two bucks trying to outmuscle and outmaneuver each other. If a buck doesn't respond in 20 or 30 minutes, there probably isn't one coming. Three or four series of antler clashing, ground pounding and tree scraping should be enough in that span of time. Try not to rattle too much.

If a buck is seen approaching but looks unsure of whether he wants to come all the way, try touching the tines together lightly. A grunt might be enough to convince him the fight is for real, too.

When getting up to leave a calling site, do so cautiously. Look all around carefully for a deer that may have been hidden from view until then. One may decide to step in the open at the last minute.

Try rattling at locations that are from one-quarter to one-half mile apart. Don't expect to attract a buck at each spot. One may show at the first stand you take, or the tenth. If calling sites are chosen carefully during the peak of the rut, the odds of collecting a buck by having him come to you are good.

To prevent antlers used for rattling from drying they can be rubbed with linseed oil or lanolin. A tree stand is not a good position from which to try to rattle up a buck. The elevated sound is unnatural.

Mouth-blown calls will attract both bucks and does. Bucks respond best during the rut. Does are likely to investigate a call any time during the fall. To does, the sound produced by a call resembles the bleat of a fawn. A buck in the rut expects to find a receptive doe when homing in on a call. Overall, results with a call are more erratic than rattling.

Deer calls are available commercially, or hunters can make their own. Some quail and predator calls available on the market work as well as those made to imitate deer. I have called in several whitetail does while using a predator call. Alaska's sitka blacktail deer are reported to be receptive to quail calls.

The simplest deer call consists of a blade of grass. It is blown on while stretched between clenched thumbs. Homemade deer calls can

Predator and quail calls sometimes attract deer as well as a conventional deer call.

be made from a rubber band and a couple of pieces of wood. The pieces should be about four inches long. Each should have matching, narrow openings in their centers. The elastic is held taut across the opening when the wood is fitted together. The ends can be taped or bound with strong thread. Indians have to be given credit for devising these two deer calls.

Calls will work any time of the day, but are most effective early and late in the day. There is more chance of a deer hearing the calls on a quiet day. Windy conditions are poor for trying to bring in deer with a call.

The same basic considerations mentioned for choosing a stand for rattling apply when situating yourself to try a call. Whitetails or mule deer drawn to the sound may come on the run or sneaking. Try blowing the call at ten-minute intervals. The technique can be varied, however. Some hunters make from one to three loud bleats at a time, others use series of three long and two short, then pause.

One of the best ways to use a call is to have it handy while still hunting. When deer are jumped and are running, a blast from a call can stop them long enough for a shot. It may even bring an animal back that has already gone out of sight, providing the buck or doe wasn't badly spooked.

A call can be used similarly while on stand. Deer that pass by without providing a shot may be lured back into view. Those that are running may be stopped by the sound of a bleat.

As with rattling, mouth-blown calls aren't likely to produce results in areas with high densities of hunters.

10

Weapons

There is no one best rifle or bow and arrow for deer hunting. There are a number of bests in each category.

Carrying it one step further, there is no one best type of weaponry for deer hunting. Rifles, both modern and muzzle-loaders, shotguns, handguns, and bow and arrow all have their advantages and advocates.

There are, however, some in each category that are better for some or all forms of deer hunting than others due to trajectory, recoil, weight, and killing power. For these reasons, and others, some in each class are more suited for deer hunting than others. Those are the ones we will be discussing.

One of the major reasons for the diversity of "bests" for deer hunting is that both mule deer and whitetails are easy to kill. More important than a firearm's or bow's power, within limits, is the hunter's ability to place his shot accurately in a vital area. A firearm or bow is often chosen to meet the individual hunter's personal needs or desires rather than for its ability to kill a deer since many can do this.

Another consideration in the line of best weapons for deer hunting is the varying types of terrain in which both muleys and whitetails are found. Rifles that are tops for deer in thick cover may be poor in open terrain and vice versa. There are some that perform equally well under a variety of circumstances, however.

Obtaining a weapon adequate for deer hunting is probably the easiest part of the pursuit. The skill to use it properly and to be consistently in a position to shoot at deer with it are much harder.

There are a number of centerfire rifle calibers that will perform adequately for all deer hunting. They include the .243, 6 mm, .25-06, .270, .280, .284, .300 Savage, .30-06, and .308. Of those, the .270 and .30-06 have to be rated the best of the lot.

My personal preference in caliber for a deer rifle is the .30-06. I bought my first one because my father had one and swore by it. Actually, that was only part of the reason. Dad said a rifle in that caliber would be satisfactory for hunting any big game in North America. What I read about the ought-six bore him out; so I was convinced. The hunting I have done with that first .30-06 and the others that followed has fortified my opinion of the caliber.

A .270 is just as good as an 06 for deer hunting. Some, usually hunters who own them, say it is better. The additional calibers mentioned don't rank far down the list from either of these two.

Some deer hunters may scoff at the thought of light calibers such as the .243 for all-around deer rifles. I once shared the opinion, but have since altered my thoughts after seeing several in action on whitetails

The author collected this buck with his favorite caliber deer rifle—a .30-06.

and mule deer. Their biggest advantage is light recoil, which often results in better accuracy, when compared with calibers that pack a more noticeable wallop. The .243, for instance, is a good choice for any deer hunter, but especially for women and youngsters.

Deer hunters shouldn't worry about the old myth that light, fast bullets are useless in brush. Such a bullet won't plow through twigs and branches that are in its way and drill a deer right where the shooter was aiming. Neither will a bullet from a rifle in any of the bigger calibers mentioned. The simple fact of the matter is that no bullet designed for deer hunting has the capability of busting through brush. Wait for an open shot and a .243 will kill a whitetail or muley as dead as a .30-06 if the bullet is placed where it should be.

What about the .30-30, .35, and .44 for deer? They are alright for hunting in areas where shots are likely to be from 50 to 100 yards maximum. Their trajectories are poor at ranges beyond that. The 7 mm and 300 magnums are bigger than necessary for deer hunting.

There are characteristics or features of a deer rifle that are more important than caliber. Chief among these are length, weight, action, and sights. The type of terrain deer are hunted in and the most often used method of hunting them will dictate which features a hunter should consider when buying a rifle.

A still-hunter or tracker, for instance, who treads in cover where shots are less than 100 yards will want a rifle that is short, light, fast-aiming and shooting. One that weighs between six and seven pounds or less, has an 18½-inch or 20-inch barrel and iron sights. A peep sight is great for quick aiming. Some who like a scope and don't mind the extra weight might want a fixed-power model or a low-power variable. The action could be lever, pump, or semiautomatic.

The deer hunter who spends a lot of time on stands or hunts country where shots average from 100 to 300 yards will want a rifle that is as accurate as possible. Weight isn't as critical here; so a rifle that weighs over seven pounds and has a 22-inch or 24-inch barrel is okay. A telescopic sight is almost a must. Any type of action would do, but bolt actions are a good choice.

An accessory rifle deer hunters should seriously consider regardless of the type of gun they have or the preferred hunting method is a sling. The straps are helpful in steadying aim and for carrying a rifle over the shoulder while climbing or dragging a deer. Slings can also be used to hang a firearm on a convenient limb during a break rather than laying it on the ground.

Many deer hunters tend to use bullets heavier than they should in their hunting. This is especially true in "brush country." Some hunters

Successful deer hunter inspects buck he just dropped with a bolt action .30-30. This caliber is popular for deer hunting, but isn't one of the best choices.

who frequent such cover in their search for deer incorrectly believe that the heavier the bullet they use, the greater their chances of hitting a deer standing on the opposite side of a thicket. Any bullet from a deer rifle that hits a branch or some other obstruction in its path will expand and deflect. Unless a deer is directly behind the obstruction that is hit, the slug is more likely to wound or miss the animal than kill it. Shots intentionally taken through branches with the hopes of hitting deer are a waste of ammunition as well as unsportsmanlike. If an opening large enough to get a bullet through does not exist, hunters shouldn't shoot.

Slugs over 150 grains are unnecessary for deer hunting. Those weighing 180 or 220 grains often do not expand properly. There have

123

been a lot of deer bagged with slugs 180 grains and larger. I have collected some myself. In many cases the projectile goes completely through the animal, inflicting less damage than a lighter bullet would. A second shot is sometimes required to finish whitetails and muleys hit with heavy bullets.

The amount of shocking power a slug delivers determines its effectiveness. A bullet that opens up and expends all of its energy inside a deer gives optimum performance. When a bullet passes through a deer, some of its shocking power is lost.

A disadvantage of heavy bullets in areas where long shots are common is their trajectory. They drop much faster than lighter slugs. According to Winchester's ballistics chart, a .30-06, 180-grain bullet drops about seven inches more than one of the same design weighing 150 grains at 300 yards.

Deer hunters who use .35s or .44s don't have any choice in bullet weight. They are stuck with 200-grain and 240-grain slugs respectively.

For the .243 and 6mm, 100-grain bullets are tops. A 120-grain slug is good for the .25-06; 130 or 150 grains in .270; 140 grains in .280; 150-grain slugs are good for the .284, .30-30, .300, .30-06 and .308. Federal introduced a 125-grain, hollow-point, .30-30 bullet in 1977. This is not designed for deer hunting! It is for predator and woodchuck hunting.

Generally, soft-point bullets are the best for deer hunting. Pointed soft-points are better than round-nose bullets when shooting at moderate to long ranges. Pointed bullets have less wind resistance and drop less than blunt slugs.

Try not to carry cartridges, not many anyway, in pockets where they will clank together. Shell holders that fit on the belt are good for carrying rifle shells. What I do is have a couple of extra shells handy, one in each pants or coat pocket. The rest of my ammunition stays in a pack I always carry when hunting.

Choosing a muzzle-loading rifle for deer hunting is a different matter than a modern gun. Percussion cap, replica muzzle-loaders are best suited for deer hunting. Flintlocks are also used successfully by some deer hunters. Rifles are available in finished models or in kits that the hunter can put together himself.

Caliber choices vary, but the most popular for deer include .44, .45, .50, .54, and .58. The minimum required caliber for deer hunting varies from state to state. Deer hunters are best off using at least a .50-caliber front-loader.

I highly recommend muzzle-loaders with double triggers. More specifically, those manufactured by Thompson/Center Arms. Only the front trigger releases the hammer. The rear one is called a set trigger.

Musket shooters sight their rifles in on a range.

When it is pulled back it reduces the amount of finger pressure required on the front trigger to fire the rifle. Muskets I have tried with single triggers required an excessive amount of finger pressure to shoot them, often resulting in poor groups.

Two basic types of projectiles are used in muzzle-loaders for hunting: round balls and maxi-balls (maxis with a concave base are often referred to as miniballs). Both are satisfactory for hunting. Some states only permit the use of round balls during special black powder deer seasons. Maxi-balls are bullet-shaped.

Round balls must be used with a patch. The conventional cloth patch must be lubricated. Cloth patches can be purchased dry or prelubricated. A commercial lubrication, such as Maxi-Lub available from Thompson/Center, should be applied to dry patches. Some musket shooters use Crisco or Vaseline on their patches, but these preparations aren't recommended in cold weather.

The proper patch thickness to use with round balls is critical. A certain amount of pressure is required to start a properly patched ball down the barrel to insure a tight fit. If so much pressure is necessary that the lead ball is deformed, the patch is too thick. If the ball slips in easily, it is too thin. Most sporting goods dealers who handle muzzle-loaders can recommend the proper size patch. There may be some variance from rifle to rifle, however; so if one thickness doesn't work right for you, try a different one.

Butler Creek Corporation from Jackson Hole, Wyoming, recently

125

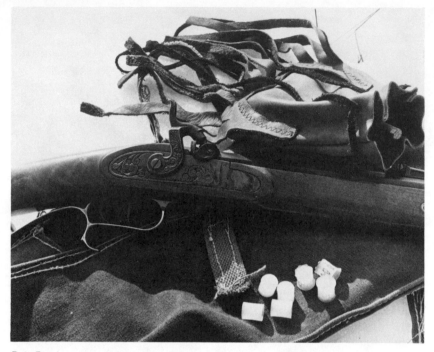

Poly-Patches are an alternative to cloth patches when shooting round balls out of a muzzle-loader. The three on the right have been fired. The author fired a tighter group using Poly-Patches than with cloth patches.

developed what they call a Poly-Patch as an alternative to cloth patches. They are plastic, cylindrical, and have a cup on both ends. I have test-fired round balls with poly patches and got tighter groups than with cloth patches.

No patch is required with maxi-balls. Lubricant is applied directly to the bullet then it is seated on top of the powder charge.

A handy rule of thumb for determining a powder charge for hunting is to multiply your rifle caliber by two. With a .50 caliber, for instance, 100 grains of powder would be adequate. That is the maximum recommended load for Thompson/Center's .50 caliber Hawken using maxi-balls and FFG powder. For round balls the top load listed in their tables is 110 grains of powder. FFG is satisfactory for use with all the calibers mentioned.

A powder designed for use in percussion muzzle-loaders (it won't work in flintlocks) that isn't a true black powder has been developed. It is called Pyrodex. Pyrodex burns cleaner than black powder, resulting in less residue in the barrel after each shot. Because it is not black powder, Pyrodex can not be used during some muzzle-loader deer seasons.

Loading a musket is easy. Before a muzzle-loader is charged, a couple of percussion caps should be fired to clear away any grease or oil that may dampen the powder charge. Once this is accomplished, rest the rifle on its butt plate with the hammer at half cock. Then measure the desired amount of powder and pour it down the barrel. Strike the barrel several times with the heel of your hand to settle the powder in the chamber.

The projectile is next, either a patch and ball or a lubricated maxi. If using a cloth patch, try to be sure it is centered on the barrel and the grain of the cloth is facing the same way at each loading. Most round balls have a sprue mark, a spot of upraised lead, this should also be centered and face up.

A starter is necessary to get a ball into the bore. Once it is several

This lucky front-loader hunter downed a nice buck with a .50 caliber Hawken made by Thompson/Center Arms.

inches down the barrel, a ramrod can be used to seat it firmly, without pounding, against the powder charge.

The base of maxi-balls can usually be started in the muzzle with finger pressure. A starter can then be used to push the bullet a short distance down the barrel. The ramrod finishes the job.

Once a satisfactory hunting load has been determined, it is a good idea to mark the ramrod at the muzzle while it is resting on a seated ball or bullet; the mark will serve as a guideline for future loads to make sure all rounds are seated at the same depth. A felt-tipped pen can be used to make the mark. A mark can also be scratched in with a knife blade.

Never use smokeless powder in a muzzle-loading rifle or shoot one unless the projectile is seated against the powder.

If it isn't daylight yet when I load my musket for deer hunting, I drop the hammer on the nipple and carry the rifle that way until daylight. At that time I cock the hammer and put a percussion cap in place. I usually squeeze the cap slightly to make sure it fits the nipple snugly. Those that fit loosely may fall off.

Whether stillhunting or on a stand in cover where deer are likely to be spotted at close range, I use the set trigger as a safety. When a shot is offered I pull the set trigger and am ready to shoot. The noisy "click-click" of cocking the hammer is enough to spook a deer if one is encountered at close range.

With the hammer back a musket can be fired, even when the front trigger isn't set. It takes more pressure to release it though. Because the rifle is capable of discharging when the hammer is cocked, I make

Here are a pair of Maxi-balls. The one on the left is unfired. One on the right brought down a deer.

sure to keep fingers and brush away from the front trigger to prevent the rifle from firing accidentally. The muzzle is always pointed in a safe direction.

If I'm with someone, simply walking through the woods to a stand or if I know any deer I see will be at least 50 yards away, I lower the hammer so it rests on the percussion cap. It is cocked when and if a deer is sighted under these circumstances.

Powder and ball can't be removed at the end of the day as conveniently as a modern cartridge if they aren't fired. Actually, they don't have to be. In most cases, a muzzle-loader is considered unloaded when the cap is removed. I have carried my musket with the same load in it for weeks without misfires. The rifle is always put in a case when I'm not in the woods and kept inside a cabin or house overnight.

When camping outside, a black powder rifle should be fired into a safe backstop at the end of the day and reloaded the next morning. Under these conditions the powder could get wet during the night. Don't wait until after dark to shoot it, however. If you do, the local game warden might pay you a visit.

A musket that needs cleaning or can't be stored safely between hunts should be discharged at the end of the hunting day, too. Be sure to shoot a muzzle loader at the end of the season. With the passage of time it can be difficult to remember a load was left in the gun and an accident could result. If in doubt whether a musket is loaded, use your ramrod—which should be marked—to check. Don't fire a cap to test it!

Some parts of the United States require shotguns for deer hunting; and in other areas where cover is exceptionally dense and shots close, they are the most practical weapons. Without question, 10-gauge and 12-gauge scatterguns are the best shotguns for deer hunting. Sixteen gauges are alright, but 20s and .410s are poor. Many states prohibit the use of .410 shotguns for deer hunting. Twelve-gauge shotguns that handle three-inch shells are better than $2^3/_4$-inch types when buckshot is used.

A shotgun for deer hunting should be as light as possible, within the gauge limitation. The action should be fast—either pump or semiautomatic—doubles are alright. Many states require that shotguns for deer hunting be plugged to limit their shell capacity to three. Buckshot patterns best out of a full-choke scattergun. Open chokes, such as modified and improved cylinder, are better for slug use. Shotguns with barrels designed specifically for slugs are the best choice for the serious shotgun deer hunter. They come with iron sights and can be fitted with a peep sight or scope.

Slugs are the best choice in ammunition for shotguns used on deer. Number one buckshot is best for hunters who are required or choose to use buckshot. The larger 00 and 0 sizes are second and third choices. Buckshot is only effective at close ranges, 40 yards maximum. For longer shots slugs should be used.

Muzzle-loading shotguns will bring a deer down, but aren't widely used.

Handguns present yet another type of firearm for deer hunters to choose from. Calibers that have been proven effective for deer are the .44, .41, and .357 magnums plus the .30 Herrett and .30-30. All except the .30 and .30-30 are available in revolvers. Thompson/Center Arms makes a single-shot pistol that handles the .30 Herrett and .30-30.

The .44 magnum is the better of the lot because of the punch it packs. This caliber's heavy recoil and loud muzzle blast prevent some shooters from shooting it accurately. If groups from a lesser caliber such as the .357 magnum are more consistent and tighter than from the .44, it is the better choice for hunting.

Ron Coleman inspects mounted head of trophy buck he collected with a .44 magnum handgun that his daughter is pointing to.

Ron Coleman points out to daughter where he hit buck with .44 magnum handgun to drop it in its tracks.

A successful handgun deer hunter from Michigan, Ron Coleman, applies red fingernail polish to his front sight to make it easier to see.

Either soft-point or semijacketed hollow-point bullets are okay for deer hunting. The .44 is available in 240-grain slugs; the .41 in 210; .357 in 158; the .30 Herrett in 130; and the .30-30 in 150-grain bullets.

It takes more practice to master a handgun than any other type of firearm I'm acquainted with, at least it does for me. Shooters who plan on hunting deer with one should familiarize themselves with his and the gun's limitations before going afield. Shooting should be done from a steady position—sitting, prone or resting against something—whenever possible.

Now, let's consider an entirely different weapon: the bow. Unlike firearms, bows are classified by pounds of pull rather than caliber. There are several types of bows available today: compounds, recurves, longbows, and crossbows. All are used for deer hunting, but compounds and recurves are the most popular. In a few years the vast majority of bowhunting for deer will be done with compounds. Crossbows are illegal for deer hunting in all but a handful of states and Canadian provinces. A trend toward the use of longbows among archers is similar to the move toward muzzle-loading firearms among gun hunters, but not nearly as widespread.

Among the three basic types of conventional bows, longbows represent the earliest and simplest design. Compounds are the most recent, and the recurve falls in the middle. Bows have come a long way. Newer models have gone beyond the realm of the simple stick and string, although the principle remains the same.

Each advancement has improved the bow's efficiency for hunting. The step from straight bows to recurves wasn't as dramatic as the jump from recurves to compounds, but it was still a step ahead. Curved design of the limbs on recurves resulted in shorter bows. Both wood and fiberglass eventually went into the manufacture of recurves, making them stronger and more efficient than the all-wood longbows. With both of these styles of bows, their peak weight is reached at full draw.

On compounds, peak weight is experienced at the beginning of the

Longbows are the earliest design of hunting bow and are still used by some hunters.

Compound bows like this four-wheeler are the most popular for hunting today. When drawn, there is a noticeable "breaking point" in the draw weight. This occurs when the pulleys "roll over."

draw. At full draw the archer is holding a fraction of the bow's peak weight. The reduction can be from 15 to 50 percent, depending upon how many pulleys the bow has. From one half to two-thirds of the way back the reduction can be felt at the bow's "breaking point." What happens at that point is the pulleys "roll over."

This feature reduces the physical effort necessary to hold the bow at full draw, which is one of the biggest advantages of the compound over recurves. More accurate shots are the end result.

Arrows released from compound bows generally travel faster, have a flatter trajectory, and have more penetration power than shafts shot from a comparable draw-weight recurve. Another advantage the more sophisticated compounds have over any previous type of bow is their draw weight can be adjusted. Some can be adjusted over a range of ten pounds of pull, others can be varied by 15 pounds.

It should come as no surprise that I recommend the compound bow for deer hunting. They are available with two, four, or six pulleys. Two-wheelers are the simplest and cheapest compound. Draw weights are generally not adjustable on these, and weight reduction is about 50 percent at full draw. The four- and six-wheelers have adjustable draw weights, but weight reduction is usually from 15 to 35 percent at full draw.

Draw-weight reduction is directly related to arrow speed. A compound that has a 50 percent weight reduction will shoot a slower arrow than one with a 35 percent weight reduction.

The limbs on most compounds are made of laminated wood and fiberglass. Some cheaper models have all fiberglass limbs. These are not the best for hunting since fiberglass expands and contracts with changes in temperature. Ray Sischo, a local archery shop owner, explained that with fiberglass limbs "one day you might have a 40-pounder and the next a 42-pounder."

Better makes of compounds have a cable and string. On cheaper models the string is replaced by cable. The compound is changing so fast that new developments will probably be added by the time you finish reading this book.

A compound that has a draw weight of at least 45 pounds is more than adequate for deer hunting. Heavier bows up to 60-pound pull are better yet, but I wouldn't recommend that a beginning bowhunter start out at 50 or 60 pounds. Shooting a bow is more physical than firing a rifle. Poor shooting habits can develop by starting out with a too heavy bow. Muscles used in drawing a bow are seldom used for anything else; consequently, they should be developed gradually.

A four- or six-wheel compound that can be adjusted from 40 to 50 or from 45 to 60 pounds is perfect for the beginning bowhunter. Two pulley models in 45-pound pull are fine. Incidentally, Georgia is the only state that doesn't currently permit the use of compound bows during their regular archery deer season. Some states have draw-weight minimums of 30-pound pull; others require at least 40 pounds. Thirty- and 40-pound pull bows will kill deer, but a 45-pounder is a much better choice for hunters—with the exception of youngsters and some women who can't handle them.

Recurve or long bows with 45-pound-pull draw weights and heavier are okay for deer hunting, too. Recurves had a couple of advantages over compounds when the newer bows first hit the market: they were cheaper and lighter in weight. In many cases recurves can still be purchased cheaper than compounds and are lighter in weight, but these considerations aren't as important as they used to be. The advantages compounds have over recurves overshadow them to some extent. The only reason many recurves have retained lower price tags than compounds is because they wouldn't sell otherwise. Some models of recurves that used to go for $60 have been reduced to as low as $15.

As with compounds, the laminated wood and fiberglass bows are superior to those of all fiberglass. Some recurves are available in take-down models. These are convenient for travel in airplanes, buses, or when packing into a remote area on horseback. Interchangeable limbs can be purchased for take-downs that vary draw weight. This feature is similar to changing weights on compounds, but it is closer to buying separate bows for each draw weight.

Recurves that are at least 60 inches long are better for deer hunting than shorter models. Recurves are usually unstrung when not in use. A bow stringer is best for this purpose. The through-the-leg method of stringing and unstringing bows is responsible for twisting limbs if not done properly. Compound bows remain strung.

Regardless of the type of bow purchased for deer hunting, be sure to get one to correspond to your draw length. An average draw length is 28 inches. Some archers only reach 26 inches, however, and others come back 30 inches or more. Draw length depends on the individual's arm length. If interested in buying your first bow for deer hunting, try to get one from a shop where personalized service is given. An alternative would be to have a knowledgeable bow hunter help you pick out a bow suited to your draw length.

Arrows are designed to match the various draw weights of bows. The proper combination of arrow and bow is important. A rifleman wouldn't think of trying to fire a .30-30 round in his .30-06. Neither

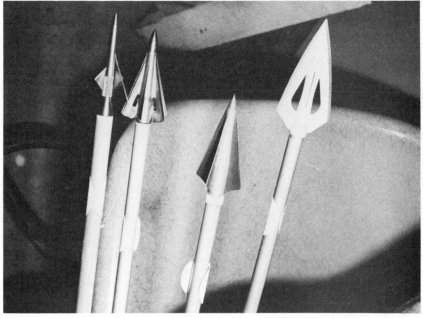

From left to right: missile spike, wasp, satellite, and Bear razorhead broadheads. The slot in the Bear head is for a razorblade insert. The missile spike is not recommended for deer hunting, nor is the wasp unless shot out of a bow with at least 50-pound pull.

should an archer consider shooting an arrow designed for a 30-pound-pull bow from his 45-pounder.

Shafts are made with a number of materials: wood, fiberglass, aluminum, and steel. Aluminum shafts are the best for hunting. Their light weight gives them a flatter trajectory than glass and steel shafts, and they aren't subject to warping like wood. Wood and fiberglass arrows are not recommended for use with compound bows.

Archery dealers who provide personalized service can tell hunters which arrows will perform best in their bow. It makes a difference whether the shafts will be used with a recurve or compound bow. Arrows with hunting heads designed for a 50-pound-pull recurve will not perform properly in a 50-pound-pull compound. With a compound, both the bow's peak and holding weight must be considered.

A variety of broadheads are adequate for deer hunting. In recent years there has been a trend toward heads on which factory-sharpened inserts are used for all the cutting edges. Such newer types as Satellites

Bear broadhead being sharpened on Razor Edge Kit. Hunting with sharp broadhead is important in bowhunting.

and Savoras are good. Wasp heads are not recommended. The Razor-back Five is a new head that promises to perform well, too.

Among the older heads that require sharpening, I prefer the Bear Razorhead. Black Diamonds and Pearson Switchblades are also good. These heads have razorblade inserts in addition to the main head with two cutting edges.

Regardless of the style of broadhead a deer hunter uses, he should make sure it is *sharp*. *Sharp* enough to shave the hair on your arm. Those that rely completely on razor inserts will be *sharp* when purchased. Other types *must be sharpened* with a file or stone. Two kits that are excellent for sharpening broadheads are on the market. One is manufactured by Razor Edge, Box 203, Butler, Wisconsin 53007. The other is available through Donald D. Moss, 2055 E. Canal, Turlock, California 95380.

Some hunting heads perform better in one type of bow than another; so be sure to try those you intend to hunt with well ahead of the season.

Plastic fletching is better for hunting arrows than feathers. Plastic doesn't get wet in rain and is also quieter. Plastic-fletched arrows must be shot from fingerlike arrow rests made of plastic or coiled wire. Feathers can be shot accurately from a shelf rest.

A quiver will be needed to carry hunting arrows. Back and bow quivers are the two basic types for hunting. I personally prefer those that can be attached directly to the bow by clamps or screws. Extra arrows are always at hand when needed. Whichever a bowhunter chooses, he should make sure the area where broadheads rest in the quiver is covered. This protects the cutting edges from getting dulled on brush as well as protecting the hunter from accidentally cutting himself.

Bow shooters will also need an armguard to protect their forearm from the occasional slap of the bowstring and to keep loose sleeves from interfering with the string. A shooting glove or tab for fingers with which to grip the string is required, too. Another of the target archer's innovations, releases, are used by some hunting archers. Mechanical releases are not legal for hunting in some states.

Mastering a bow and arrow takes more time and practice than ma-

The arrow this archer is retrieving after a miss will have to be sharpened before it is used again because it will have been dulled by rocks and sand. Note the back quiver this hunter is carrying. It is covered with deer hide to make it quiet.

stering firearms. Nonetheless, the effort can be well worthwhile. Hunting deer with archery equipment can be more satisfying and challenging than hunting with any other weapon. Bow deer seasons are often longer than firearms hunts, which increases the hunter's time afield. One of the best ways to learn how to shoot a bow and arrow properly is to read all you can on the subject and join a local archery club. Established shooters are always more than willing to give beginners pointers.

Bows don't normally require much attention to keep them in working order. The pulleys on compounds can be oiled occasionally, but that is about it. A light coating once a year should do the trick. Broadheads can be protected from rust by coating them with Vaseline.

Firearms should be cleaned on a regular basis, especially black powder guns. The barrels of muzzle-loading rifles pick up so much residue that loading them becomes difficult after they have been fired a

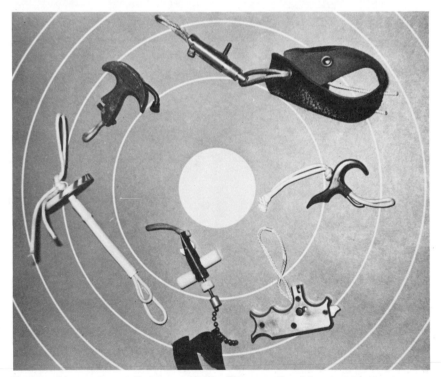

Variety of bow releases that are available. They are illegal for deer hunting in some states.

Author runs hot water through muzzle-loader barrel, the first step in cleaning. Rag around the barrel protects hand from the heat.

number of times. Dirty barrels aren't as much of a problem with modern rifles, shotguns, and handguns, but they still require care.

My dad impressed his two boys with the importance of gun care as soon as they were old enough to hunt. After returning home from a day of hunting we had to look after our guns before anything else. If they had been fired, barrels were cleaned inside and wiped with an oily rag on the outside. Unfired guns were simply wiped down and then put away. The procedure took a matter of minutes.

I still believe it is a good idea to look after a gun each time it is used, especially if it is wet from rain or snow. After wet days in the field, barrels should be cleaned even if the gun wasn't fired during the day. Sometimes moisture gets in at the muzzle. A good way to keep rain and snow out of the barrel of a deer gun is to put a piece of tape or cellophane over the muzzle (use a rubber band to hold it on). This doesn't affect accuracy and isn't dangerous.

To clean the barrel of a modern gun simply run a wire brush with solvent on it through, then wipe clean with a couple of patches. Try to wipe all exposed metal parts with an oily rag before putting guns away.

Musket barrels must be cleaned with hot, soapy water (a mild soap such as Ivory is good). What I usually do is pour a pitcher of hot water down my musket barrel. That drains a lot of the black powder residue. Then I submerge the nipple end in a bucket of soapy water and work a 12-gauge shotgun-cleaning rod with a patch up and down. Once the barrel is clean I use two or three patches to dry it completely.

A light coating of oil goes on the exterior surfaces of the gun. After cleaning is complete, I usually snap a couple of percussion caps to make sure the barrel is dry.

When deer hunting away from home, try to remember to bring a gun-cleaning kit along.

11

Sights

Sights are an integral part of any gun and many bows used for deer hunting.

For firearms there are two basic types of sights: iron and telescopic. Scopes are the most widely used because of their adaptability for many hunting situations. They have several advantages over iron sights: target and sights are visible on one plane; the target is usually magnified and scopes have the ability to gather light under poor light conditions. Most scope eyepieces are circular, but wide field models that are oblong are also available.

The field of view a hunter has through a scope decreases as its magnification increases. For this reason low powers from 1.5X to 4X are best for close shots and finding running deer in the glass. Higher magnifications are best used for medium- to long-range shots and looking for antlers on deer that can't be seen clearly with the naked eye.

Telescopic sights are available in either fixed power or variable models with a selection of reticles. Variables are the most versatile. The selection of variables includes 1.5X-4X, 2.5X-7X and 3X-9X. For hunters who do a lot of still-hunting and tracking or want a scope for their shotgun, the low-power variable is tops. Stand hunters who frequent open country would be better off with the higher magnification variables.

When hunting it is best to keep variables on the lowest power. If a deer is spotted that you want to get a better look at, crank up the power then. Try to remember to crank it back down after the higher magnification is no longer needed. I made the mistake of not doing that one time and missed a buck because of it.

While on a stand I spotted a deer about 150 yards away. I cranked the power on my 3x all the way up to 9x to look at its head. It was a doe. Sometime later a buck came hotfotting by me no more than 30 yards away. My field of view was so small at that range with the scope still on nine power I couldn't find him in it. He was out of sight before I realized what the problem was.

Fixed-power scopes are generally cheaper than variables. Good choices for rifles or shotguns are 2X, 2.5X, or 4X. Handgun scopes come in 1.3X, 1.7X, and 2.5X.

Crosshairs are the most popular scope reticle. The duplex or tapered variety ranks on top, followed by coarse crosshairs and dot types. Fine crosshairs are difficult to see in poor light, which makes them a poor choice for deer hunting.

Scope covers are a must for rainy or snowy days. I prefer see-throughs that permit aiming with them in place. I leave them on all the time. A magazine article I read recently said using clear lens covers is a bad idea, however. It said they reduce image clarity, light gathering qualities of the scope, and more important, change point of impact. I haven't noticed any problems with my scoped rifles on which the caps were used; maybe because they were sighted in with the covers in place. Hunters should test the accuracy of their scopes both with covers on and off to see if there is a difference if they wish to use clear types. In the event poorer results are achieved with covers in place, plan on removing them to shoot whenever possible. Remember clear caps are not made for quick, easy removal.

Lens covers for scopes that are designed to flip up and out of the way with the touch of a finger are the fastest to remove. They are manufactured by Butler Creek Corporation, P.O. Box GG, Jackson Hole, Wyoming 83001. These aren't available in a see-through style.

The type of rifle or shotgun a scope is put on dictates whether it will be mounted on the side or on top. Beyond that there are mounts that flip to the side, those that are mounted high so iron sights can be seen under them, low mounts, and those that can be quickly detached. One mount is as good as another as long as they are solidly anchored and the shooter can see through the scope properly.

I use low mounts that can't be quickly detached. The reason is I have faith in the scopes on my rifles. They have never let me down. The incident mentioned earlier about not getting a shot at a buck because my scope was on high power was my fault, not the scope's. The only situation I've encountered where a scope would have been useless if a shot were offered is when looking directly into the sun. I always avoid putting myself in a position where aiming at a deer into the sun would be required.

I will admit scope mounts that provide for quick conversion to iron-sight use have their place. If something happened to a scope on a hunting trip rendering it temporarily or permanently useless, such a mount would prove invaluable. Fortunately, I haven't been in such a situation. On deer hunting trips away from home I sometimes carry a spare rifle.

Scope users who have flip-over or quick detachable mounts should make sure the scope is flipped back or remounted the way it originally was after using iron sights. If it isn't aligned properly, the point of impact will be changed and the next shot taken with the scope probably won't go where it ought to. Marks of some sort can be used as guidelines to make sure the scope is always repositioned properly.

It is best to have a gunsmith or dealer mount a scope unless you have done it before. Set screws must be cinched down tight so recoil won't jar them loose. If you do the mounting yourself, use a screwdriver that fits the screws properly. Also, put some Loctite or varnish on the screw threads just before putting them in as added insurance against them loosening.

Last year one of my brothers-in-law, Bruce Dupras, bought a new rifle and scope. I advised him to have a local sport shop mount the scope. He didn't listen. Bruce went through more than a box of shells on his first trip to the range trying to sight in his rifle before he realized the scope was loose.

Most rifles and handguns come with iron or open sights. Hunters who can't afford a scope are stuck with them. They are not all that bad though. Some deer hunters even prefer iron sights over the telescopic variety. A rifle is lighter with iron than glass, and in many cases can be aimed faster. Iron sights are not made for long range shooting, however. They perform best on deer at distances under 100 yards.

In my opinion, a receiver or peep sight is superior to the conventional rear sight for deer hunting. The eye automatically centers the front sight in the aperture for accurate, quick sighting. Since the peep is close to the eye, it will be out of focus, as it should be; and the shooter will have only two planes to try to focus on (the front sight and target) as opposed to three points of focus when a conventional rear sight is used. Additionally, peep sights don't block parts of deer from the shooter's view as other rear sights do.

It is best to unscrew the eyepiece on peep sights and use the larger hole for hunting.

Here are two types of receiver or peep sights. They are great for quick aiming.

Rear sights that are standard equipment on rifles and handguns vary, but most are notched in the shape of a U or V. The U on some sights is squared off; others are rounded. I prefer a notch as small as possible in the round-bottomed U. Rear sights that have a triangular-shaped mark on the surface facing the shooter make it easier to find the center for aligning the front sight.

Front sights come in bead, blade, or post varieties. I like the bead. Some front sights are covered with hoods to block out side lighting. I don't like them because they reduce light in low-light situations. Hoods are also distracting to me. They can usually be slipped off easily.

Whey buying a gun with iron sights, try aiming it to see if the sight picture is satisfactory. If not, look for a different firearm. Regardless of the other qualities a rifle, handgun, or slug-barreled shotgun may possess, its effectiveness will be minimized if the sights are less than adequate for your use.

Some bowhunters don't use sights. They shoot instinctively in a fashion similar to the way a shotgunner points his gun, or the tip of their broadhead is used as a point of reference for aiming. Many archers use sights, however, as evidenced by the increasing variety of bow sights on the market. There are pins, scopes, peeps, rangefinders, and lighted sights.

As a gun hunter turned archer, I prefer a sight on my bow. It helps me to pick out a spot on a deer rather than shooting at the whole animal. Sights are especially valuable for shooting at distances beyond

30 yards. Some bowhunters shoot instinctively at ranges under 30 yards, but rely on a sight for longer shots.

Due to the poor trajectory of an arrow as compared to a rifle bullet, multiple aiming points are available on most sights. A series of pins are the most common and, I think, the best for deer hunting. The pins are usually set for distances in increments of ten yards. If a bowhunter restricts his shots at deer to within 30 years, he may only need one or two pins.

A rear sight isn't necessary for aiming with a bow. Archers draw to the same anchor point (a corner of the mouth is the most commonly

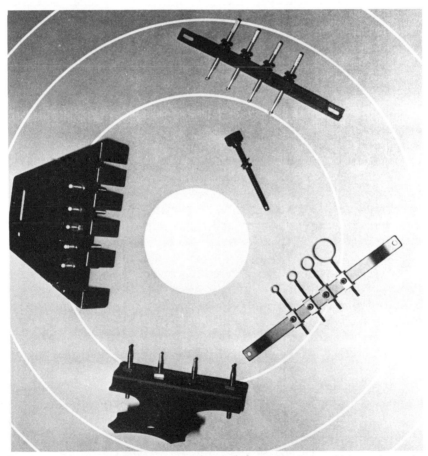

The best type of bowsight for hunting incorporates a series of pins which can be set for various yardages. The sight with rings is a rangefinder model and the single pin in the middle is a lighted sight.

used) for every shot, which results in a consistent sight picture. Some bow shooters do use peep sights. These sights fit between strands on the bowstring. Peeps make precision shooting possible and are used primarily by target archers.

Another feature on bows that allows for a consistent sight picture are nocking points. Metal "stops" are clamped on the string, usually at a point from $3/8$ to $1/2$ inch above the arrow rest, to mark nocking points. Arrow nocks fit on the string directly under the nocking point.

Telescopic sights made for bows were also designed for target shooters, but can be used for hunting. They come in two, four, and six power. Rangefinder sights are helpful to bow hunters if they have difficulty estimating distances accurately in the field. Sometimes there isn't time to use them though. Lighted bow sights are advantageous for seeing point-of-aim under poor light conditions.

As with any other type of sight, try to pick one for your bow that you will be happy with. Test several varieties if possible. Sights that can be securely fastened to a bow with screws are a better choice than those that must be taped in place.

Sights have to be aligned so the bullet or arrow hits where they are aimed before they will do the gun or bowhunter any good. Most iron sights are reasonably accurate as they come from the factory. Scopes mounted by dealers are usually bore-sighted. Nonetheless, be sure to shoot the rifle, shotgun, or handgun yourself to adjust the sights for your eyes and desired sight-in distance. Do it as far in advance of the opening of deer season as possible, especially in the case of a brand-new gun. Problems with guns and sights don't develop often, but if they do they should be recognized as soon as possible so they can be corrected.

One year a friend of mine ordered a deer-hunting rifle on which the firing pin broke after several rounds were fired. Fortunately, he got it months before the season and was able to get a rifle to hunt with to replace the faulty one.

Hunters who don't have access to a regular range to sight in their gun should select a location with an adequate backstop. State and provincial departments of natural resources or fish and game usually have certain areas designated for target practice. Targets can be pinned to cardboard boxes. I usually use a paper plate for a target. If shooting a scoped gun, a circular aiming point is colored in the center with a crayon or felt-tipped pen. A heavy cross is used as an aiming point for iron sights. The front sight often completely covers a circle.

When shooting a gun or sight you are not familiar with, do not start out with the target far away. If the sights are way out of whack, your bullets may hit off the paper at those distances. It is best to fire the first rounds at a target no further than 25 yards away. Once the gun is on target at close range it can be fine-tuned for longer ranges.

Always shoot from the steadiest position possible when sighting in a rifle. The same goes for hunting. A benchrest where the shooter can sit down and prop his gun stock on sand bags is best. Trees, vehicles, or posts are also helpful in steadying a rifle or handgun. Try to use something such as a firm cushion, tightly rolled sleep bag or sand bag to rest the gun stock on when shooting from a vehicle. The prone position with a rest is also good for accurate placement of shots. A notched cardboard or wooden box makes a good rest for shooting prone.

Slings increase accuracy from a sitting or offhand position. To get into a sling if you shoot right-handed, slip your left arm through with the rifle pointed upward and bring the strap as far back as it will go under your arm. As the rifle is lowered twist the left hand back and through the sling again. Grip the foreend so the strap lays across the back of the hand. The strap should feel tight across the chest. If it is loose, pull the left hand back. When using a sling in a sitting position, legs should be spread so elbows can rest on knees.

Some sort of ear protection, plugs or muffs, are invaluable for target practice.

When sighting in a firearm, sight adjustments should be made on the basis of three-shot groups. The center of the group should be the point of correction. Telescopic sights are the easiest to sight in. The simplest way to align the crosshairs is to move them to the center of the group by turning windage and elevation knobs. To do this, the gun must be resting solidly with sand bags under the butt and your forearm or lying in a notched box.

Gun and scope should remain in the same position throughout the process. First, fire three shots with the crosshairs on the bull's-eye. Then check to see where the center of the group is. If magnification of the scope isn't great enough to see the center, darken the spot with a pen or crayon. Next, turn windage and elevation knobs while looking through the glass so the crosshairs move across the target to that point.

Once the adjustments are complete, another group should be fired to test accuracy of the new setting. If the procedure is done properly, slugs should hit close to where they are aimed.

To get consistent groups, try to squeeze the trigger on each shot. If shots are erratic one of several things are probably happening. Either the shooter is jerking the trigger, his position isn't steady, or the scope is not mounted solidly. Set screws can work loose from the recoil of one or two rounds if they aren't installed properly. It sometimes helps

With his scoped rifle in a notched cardboard box this hunter is moving crosshairs to the center of his three-shot group to sight it in.

me to get the feel of a trigger by dry-firing a gun several times before loading the firearm.

When holding a scoped gun in a steady position isn't possible, sight correction will have to be determined by measurements. Once a group has been fired, measure the distance from its center to the center of the bull. Then scope adjustment dials can be turned an appropriate number of clicks or marks. Each calibration usually represents a shift in point of impact of an inch or less at 100 yards. How the dials are calibrated is usually specified inside dial covers, on the dials, or in the instructions that come with the scope.

Some scope adjustments are calibrated in minutes of angle. Don't let that confuse you. If each mark moves point-of-impact one minute of angle, at 100 yards point of impact will be shifted one inch. The shift will only be one-half inch at 50 yards and one-fourth inch at 25 yards.

Let's look at an example. Say the center of your group was two inches high and $3^1/_2$ inches to the right at 25 yards and your scope adjustments are calibrated in half minutes of angle (that means each mark moves point-of-impact one-half inch at 100 yards). At 25 yards the shift would be one-fourth of that or one-eighth of an inch. To adjust the crosshairs the elevation knob would have to be turned 16 clicks down (eight per inch) and the windage dial 28 to the left.

Iron sights are most often adjusted by moving the rear one whether it is a peep or the notched variety. Many types are designed to make changes to both windage and elevation easy. Set screws often control them. Some older styles of iron sights (there are still plenty of them in use) simply made allowances for shifts in elevation. Physical violence was necessary to adjust for windage by pounding them (either front or rear right or left) with a punch made of copper, brass, or nylon and a soft mallet. Shims of varying widths were required under one side or the other of some peep sights to change their right/left attitude.

It isn't as easy to determine exactly how far to move open sights as it is with scopes. The best approach is to shoot a group and make moderate corrections if any are necessary. If the next group is still off, the shooter should have a good idea how much to move the sights a second time to finalize adjustments.

Point-of-impact will shift the same direction the rear sight is moved. If the center of a group is high, for example, the rear sight must be lowered. When grouping to the right, the rear sight should be moved to the left. A change in the front sight will move point of impact the opposite direction. If the bead is moved left, bullets will hit further to the right than they did before the adjustment.

Aligning a bow sight works the same way as adjusting the front sight of a gun. The general rule is to "follow the arrow." In other words, if your arrows are grouping to the left of center, the sight should be

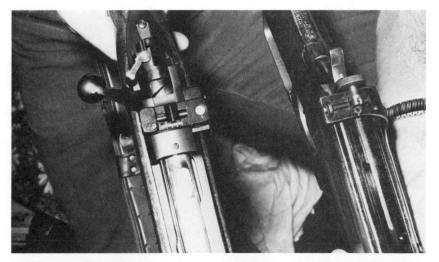

These peep sights have adjustments for both windage and elevation. Some older models just had elevation adjustments.

moved to the left. Point-of-impact will be moved to the right. If arrows hit high, raise the sight and the following shafts will strike lower.

Bow sights can be moved accidentally or jarred out of place easier than gun sights. I have found that it is beneficial to mark the positions of pins once set for desired yardages. Then if they are moved, they can be easily repositioned.

Peep sights for bows are situated on the string in a position that will conform to the shooter's eye at full draw.

Most guns or bows only have to be sighted in once, as long as the same loads and shafts are used. Alignment of the sights should be checked every year before hunting season, however, just as a precaution. Your eyes may have changed in the course of a year or something could have happened to the sights.

Always sight a gun or bow in with the very same shells, load, and arrows you will be hunting with. A change in brand, bullet weight, powder charge, shaft composition, or type of broadhead will change the point of impact.

Deer rifles used in brush country should be sighted in for 100 yards. Longer sight-in ranges, 150 or 200 yards, should be considered for hunting open terrain. Shotgunners who use slugs, musket shooters, and handgunners may want to sight in for 50 or 75 yards. Maximum yardages most bowhunters ready sights for are from 50 to 60 yards. They will also have pins set for closer distances. Gun hunters should

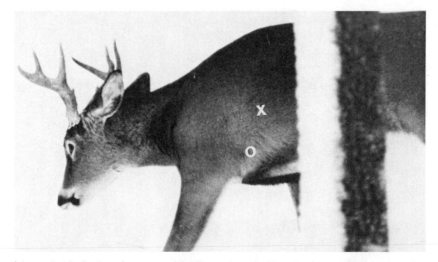

A lung shot is the best for sure, quick kills on deer. An X marks the spot for a lung hit. The heart is low in the chest where circle is.

Here is where to aim on a deer angling toward you *(photo credit: Bob Landis)*

know where their bullets, round balls, or slugs hit at a variety of ranges, too. Ballistics tables available from ammunition manufacturers give shooters a good idea how much bullet drop to expect at distances beyond 100 yards if test-firing at those yardages isn't possible.

Hunters who use buckshot in a shotgun with a simple sight plane may laugh at the idea of sighting-in with their loads. True, sight adjustment isn't possible, but some shotguns pattern high, low, left, or right of center. If so, the situation can be compensated for when shooting at a deer. Buckshot users will have to try their loads on paper to determine what kind of a pattern they are getting. Several types of buckshot should be test fired on targets to see which one gives the tightest pattern.

All deer hunters should be aware that shots taken at an uphill or downhill angle are different from those taken on a level. Bullets and arrows have a tendency to hit higher than normal when shooting either up or down. Exactly how much higher depends on the circumstances. It is a good idea to try some shots uphill or downhill to get a feel for the situation.

One of the first mule deer I shot was at a steep downhill angle. The buck was bedded about 200 yards below me. To compensate for the angle, I held the crosshairs low on his shoulder and squeezed a shot off. He jumped to his feet at the shot, apparently untouched. I held lower on the second shot and could see daylight between my crosshairs and the bottom of his shoulder when I touched it off. That one broke his back!

The time taken to learn where a gun or bow will hit at various distances and under different circumstances gives deer hunters confidence that will help when a shot is offered at a whitetail or mule deer. There won't be a bull's-eye or X to mark a spot to aim at though. Hunters will have to know what point of the anatomy to try for. The spot where a hit will bring the surest, cleanest kill.

Without question, the best all-around hit on a deer is in the lungs. This is because they are vital organs, present a relatively large target, and their location is easy to determine. A deer hit in the lungs with a projectile from any of the weapons discussed in this book is not going to go far.

The lungs fill a large part of the chest cavity. On broadside to slightly angling away shots, aim for a spot directly behind the front leg in the middle of the body. Even if the shot strays one way or the other, the hit will be fatal. A bullet or arrow that enters behind the front leg will ruin no meat. Shot placement on whitetails or mule deer that are angling away at a sharp angle should also be placed in the middle of the body and behind the front leg, on a line with the opposite shoulder.

Bowhunters should try for the back of the neck on deer facing directly away from them, unless the hunter is in an elevated stand. From a tree, all hunters should attempt to hit between a deer's shoulder blades in the middle of the back. The backbone will be broken if you are on target; the lungs are to either side.

This buck won't go far, if at all, if hit behind the shoulder where the X is. This hit will not ruin meat.

A hit at either of these spots should bring this buck down for keeps.

Ground-based gun hunters can bring a deer down by hitting between the hams below the base of the tail. This shot is only recommended for long guns with good penetration power.

My brother, Bruce, dropped a dandy eight-point whitetail with a rear-end shot one year. Bruce missed an angling shot first, but when the buck turned straight away he was on target. His 150-grain .30-30 slug piled the deer up on the spot. The bullet ranged forward into the lungs. There wasn't a speck of meat ruined either.

Hunters faced with shots at whitetail or mule deer angling toward them should try for the area between the shoulder and chest.

When a deer is facing the hunter, aim for the base of the neck. A shot that goes high will very likely break the animal's neck. An arrow that strikes too low here might hit the brisket, which could cause little or no damage. It is a different story if the shaft slips in on either side of the brisket. A low hit with lead isn't as critical as with an arrow.

A heart shot is always fatal, but in contrast to the lungs, the heart is a small target. The heart is lower in the chest than most hunters realize, too. There is a crease of skin on the back of the front leg where it joins the body that is supposed to be a good aiming point for those who want to try for the heart.

Properly placed neck shots kill immediately. The only problem here is that the strike zone is narrow. A hit to either side of the vertebrae can wound.

Intentionally aiming at the head is worse than trying for the neck. A deer's brain is small, the potential for wounding great.

Approach a downed deer with care. Be sure it is dead.

Whenever taking a shot at a deer, do so from the steadiest position possible. If there is time, use a rest. At least try to shoot from a sitting position. A sling helps steady aim.

If your sights are on, if you know where to aim, and if you can hit where you aim, you will get that whitetail or mule deer. Each of these considerations is as important as the others. They all must come together to make consistent kills.

Hunters should always be sure a deer that is down is dead before dropping their guard. If the whitetail or muley shows any signs of life, shoot again. If you are close to the animal, a neck shot is best. It is better to be safe than sorry. I've heard too many accounts of supposedly dead deer getting up and running off. A dead deer's eyes will be dull, lifeless, and open.

12

Cameras

An adequate camera and lens can make deer hunting a year-round pursuit. There are no seasons, bag limits, or sex restrictions to follow when you are after deer with a camera. Camera hunters don't even need a license.

Camera hunting is a logical offshoot for bowhunters or gun hunters interested in "shooting" deer during winter, spring, and summer. A camera is the only "weapon" available to individuals who want to bag whitetail and mule deer without killing the animals.

Deer hunting with a camera is every bit as challenging as trying for one with bow and arrow. Best results with both are obtained at close range. For this reason the camera user often has to be a skillful hunter, at least when after wild deer. Penned, caged, or tame whitetails and muleys are fair game for deer-fancying shutterbugs, too. Hunting skill isn't necessary to get within range of these animals.

Single-lens reflex (SLR) 35 mm cameras are the best choice for photographing deer. The photographer sees exactly what he is shooting with a 35 mm because viewing is done through the lens. It is similar to looking through a rifle scope. Most other cameras have viewfinders offset from lenses. These will be discussed later in this chapter.

Twin-lens reflex (TLR) cameras can also be used for capturing deer on film. As the name implies, these cameras have two lenses. One is for viewing and focusing, the other for taking photos. Twin-lens cameras are generally heavier, more awkward, and slower than 35s.

Author uses this 300 mm telephoto on a 35 mm single-lens reflex camera to capture many deer on film.

SLR and TLR cameras have one feature in common that makes them suitable for hunting deer: they can be fitted with a variety of lenses. Lenses range from wide-angles to telephotos. Wide-angle lenses make subjects look further away and smaller than they do to the naked eye. Telephotos increase the size or magnify subjects and bring them closer. A normal lens is the same magnification as the human eye. In other words, a subject viewed through a normal lens will appear approximately the same as it would without looking through a camera.

Normal lenses for 35 mm cameras are usually 50 mm. A 25 mm wide-angle would decrease the size of subjects by one-half. Such a lens will also make the subject look twice as far away as when viewed with a normal lens. A telephoto that is 200 mm will magnify subjects four times and make them look closer.

Cameras other than SLRs and TLRs usually come with unremoveable lenses. They are often wide-angle or normal magnification. Telephoto lenses are musts for obtaining satisfactory photos of deer. The most popular sizes for "shooting" deer are 135, 200, 300, and 400. Lenses can be purchased that have either fixed magnifications or a range of magnifications. The latter types are called zoom lenses.

Before getting into lenses further let's take a closer look at 35 mm SLR cameras in general. To beginning photographers, especially those familiar with Instamatics, SLRs often look complicated. The various numbered dials give them that appearance. Actually, 35s are not difficult to use.

It sometimes helps to consider the lens and camera body as separate entities. The only operation to worry about on the camera body itself, besides advancing the film and pressing the shutter, is setting shutter speed. Shutter speed is controlled by a dial with numbers on it that generally increase by a multiplication factor of two: 2, 4, 8, 16, 30, 60, 125, 250, and 500. Some cameras go as high as 1,000.

These numbers represent the time it takes for the camera shutter to open and close. They represent fractions of a second. A setting of 60, for instance, represents a shutter speed of 1/60 of a second and 250 is 1/250 of a second. The bigger the number, the faster the shutter speed. Which setting to use depends on the subject, assuming there is sufficient light. A moderate shutter speed of 60 or 125 is fine if the subject is stationary or moving slowly. Faster shutter speeds, 250 and 500, are useful to stop the action when the subject is in motion.

There are two adjustments that must be made on camera lenses in preparation for taking pictures. The first is setting the diaphragm opening. Diaphragms can be opened or closed to adjust for varying light conditions. There is a moveable ring around each lens which controls diaphragm openings. Each aperture is designated by a number on the ring called an f stop. The smaller the number, the larger the diaphragm opening will be.

Sixteen, for example, indicates a small opening. On the other hand, the number 1.8 reflects a large aperture. In effect, the amount of light present will determine what f stop should be used. Small-numbered f stops are best for days when light is poor and large numbered stops are appropriate for bright days.

The other adjustment necessary on lenses is focus. Focusing is accomplished by looking through the viewfinder and turning the focus ring until the image is clear.

With camera body and lens together, taking a picture can be broken down into five steps: 1, cock the camera; 2, set the shutter speed; 3, adjust the f stop (most SLRs have light-metering systems to enable the photographer to select the proper f stop); 4, focus; 5, release the shutter.

There are a variety of reliable SLR cameras and lenses on the market. I use Canon bodies and Bushnell lenses. Pentax, Nikon, and Minolta are other good makes. Good deals can usually be obtained on used equipment. When buying a new camera don't expect quality performance from the cheapest one on store shelves.

Now that the basics of using SLRs are out of the way let's get back to telephoto lenses. As the lenses increase in magnification their light-gathering ability decreases. The light-gathering ability of a lens is determined by the smallest number f stop the diaphragm will open to. Most 135 mm lenses have a maximum diaphragm opening of 2.8; 200s, 3.5; 300s, 5.5 or 5.6; and 400s, 6.3. A zoom lens, 90-230 mm made by Bushnell has a maximum of f 4.5. Therefore, 135 mm lenses can be used in situations where light conditions are poor, and the lighting has to be good where 400 mm lenses are employed.

My two favorites in telephotos are the 135 and 300. Some photographers who regularly shoot deer swear by 400s, and even 600s.

Lens extendors called doublers can be used to double the magnification of telephotos. Doublers fit between the camera body and regular lens. Those I have used yielded poor results. Extremely good light is necessary to use lens extendors because they reduce the light-gathering ability of lenses.

The weight of telephoto lenses increases in proportion to magnification. A 300 mm is generally heavier than a 200 mm, and a 400 mm is heavier than either of the others. This is an important consideration when it comes to taking photos of deer. The heavier a lens is the less likely it is that a photographer will be able to take good pictures when holding camera and lens by hand. Weight induces wobbling, which blurs pictures.

Fast shutter speeds are often enough to offset the jiggles caused by hand-holding a telephoto. It is even better to rest a camera mounted with a long lens against a tree, fence post, car, or anything else to steady it. A tripod is better yet for shooting with telephotos. Tripods enable camera deer hunters to get satisfactory shots of deer with a telephoto at low shutter speeds that are sometimes necessary in the morning and evening when light is poor.

A couple of general rules that apply to shooting deer with a camera are: use a tripod whenever possible and shoot at the fastest shutter speed the available light will allow. Try to press the shutter release smoothly, too, as you would squeeze the trigger of a rifle. Punching the release will increase the chances of camera movement, which can blur pictures.

Always try to focus on the eyes of a deer before taking its picture. The eyes are the center of attention. If they are in focus, the photo will be acceptable. And above all else, take a number of exposures of your subject. Don't be satisfied with one or two shots. Those extra ex-

Telephoto lenses magnify subjects and make them look closer. Always try to focus on a deer's eye.

posures can make the difference between mediocre and excellent results. It only takes one good shot to make a photo session with deer worthwhile in terms of getting a "trophy." The one you didn't take may have been the best.

Vary your exposure, too. Light meters sometimes read the background rather than the subject. This is especially true when shooting with snow, water, or sky in the background. If time permits, take a couple of exposures on what appears to be the right setting; then take a couple each at one stop over and one stop under that. This is called bracketing. It almost guarantees that at least a pair of shots will be properly exposed. Sometimes underexposed or overexposed subjects produce interesting effects. Silhouettes are prime examples of underexposed photos that can be appealing.

A beginning camera hunter shouldn't expect to get topnotch results the first time out. Becoming proficient with a camera takes practice, just as proficiency with a gun or bow and arrow does. Zoos are perfect practice ranges for deer photographers. Try to expose several rolls of film at a zoo before heading in the field. It helps to jot down f stops and shutter speeds used during practice sessions to evaluate the results when the film is developed.

Overexposed pictures are the result of too much light striking the film. Underexposures mean there wasn't enough light. Fuzzy or blurred photos are the result of poor focusing or camera movement caused by a too slow shutter speed or an unsteady lens.

Unlike hunting with gun or bow, success with a camera is subject to the users interpretation. Deer successfully bagged with a bullet or arrow are dead. There is no in-between. Images of deer shot with a camera are imprinted on film. The images can be distant, close-up, in focus, out of focus, fuzzy, sharp, underexposed, overexposed, or a combination of these.

From my point of view, I would consider a photo of a whitetail or mule deer that was in focus, sharp, properly exposed, and reasonably close a successful shot. Anything else would be a miss. I can remember times, however, when I was happy with any image of a deer on film.

The quality of a photo isn't the only factor that determines its value to the photographer. Memories that go with it add their special appeal to exposures of deer. A photo or slide that is poor quality may be valuable (a trophy) if it brings to mind pleasant or humorous memories of the circumstances under which the shot was obtained.

There is a setting on SLR cameras that I should mention now. It deals with the type of film used. Film is rated according to ASA, which refers to its light absorbing properties. Low-numbered ASA films require more light to expose properly than high-numbered ASA films. Low ASA films exhibit less grain and usually give better quality enlargements than high ASA films.

Color slide film is the best for use for photographing deer. It is cheaper to have processed than print film. Additionally, prints, both black and white and color, can be made from good slides. Kodak slide

Author focuses on deer in preparation for taking photo of himself with his kill.

film comes in ASA 25, 64, and 200. The 200 film can also be used at 400 ASA.

Kodak film is about the best made. They make Kodachrome and Ektachrome slide film. Kodachrome accents reds. Ektachrome is a blue film. Kodachrome only comes in ASA 25 and 64. The Ektachromes are available in 64, 200, and 400. I use Kodachrome 64 more than any other type, but always carry Ektachrome 200 for use in low-light situations.

The ASA dial on 35 mm cameras should be set to correspond with the film being used. This adjusts the camera's light meter.

Try to load film in your camera properly. Instructions that come with the film will explain how. Before closing the camera cover make sure the film advances as it is supposed to by pressing the shutter and cocking the camera. The rewind knob should turn when advancing the film after taking several exposures. If it doesn't, the film isn't advancing.

Hunters who are successful in bagging a deer during the fall hunting season frequently want to get pictures of themselves with their kill. SLR 35s with a normal or wide angle lens are fine for this use. Other cameras, such as Instamatics and rangefinder 35s, can also be used in these situations.

It isn't possible to look through the lens or interchange lenses with rangefinder 35 mm cameras. Otherwise their use is similar to SLRs. Some rangefinders have automatic lighting adjustments and crude focusing systems, too.

162

Instamatics are the simplest cameras to use, even though some models are rather sophisticated. All there is to do with these is center the subject in the viewfinder and shoot. Polaroid cameras are also easy to use, but they seldom function properly outside, except when the weather is warm.

The best deer kill photos are available immediately after the kill; so hunters should try to carry a camera with them. The happy expression of a successful deer hunter is bound to be more appealing at that time than a forced grin later. A natural setting also adds a great deal more to such a picture than a cluttered yard, basement, or a deer-on-the-car pose.

Try to get in close for photos of hunters with their deer. Close-ups are often more dramatic than exposures taken from a distance that lack detail. Too much background can detract from the subject. Before tak-

Photo taken with cable-released camera. Shot would have been better if stalks of grass had been removed and hat brim had been lifted. Deer's tongue should have been put in mouth.

Author took this photo of himself approaching a young buck he got with bow and arrow.

163

ing close-ups, remember to make sure the deer's tongue is in its mouth. Wiping off excess blood will make the photo look less gruesome, too.

Due to the poor light conditions whitetails and muleys are frequently shot in, it is a good idea to carry a flash attachment or flash cubes. Without them it might not be possible to capture that happy moment on film.

Deer hunters who are alone when they make a kill can still get photos. Some Instamatics and most 35s have self-timers or can be fitted with a cable release to take self-portraits. Simply set the deer up where you want it, leaving room for yourself in front or behind the animal. Use a stick with a hat on it as a dummy for yourself. The camera can be set on a tripod, rock, or stump.

Focus either on the deer or hat, then get in position. Self-timers usually give the hunter five seconds to get set from the time the shutter release is pushed. Cable releases allow the photographer to take exposures from where he wants to be. A 30-foot, air-bulb release is best for this use. When a cable release is used the tubing should be kept out of the picture. It can be hidden in grass, brush, or leaves. An alternative is to set the camera so the ground will be excluded from the shot. The best way to squeeze the bulb and release the shutter is by stepping or kneeling on it. This leaves both hands free.

Several things to keep in mind when taking shots of yourself are: make sure no obstructions like grass or twigs obscure any part of the deer or yourself; when wearing a hat or cap, tip the brim up so it doesn't shade your face; and take a number of exposures at different f stops to make sure the exposure will be correct.

13

Clothing and Equipment

Your effectiveness as a deer hunter will be determined, in part, by your comfort, which is directly related to the clothes you wear. The type and amount of clothing a deer hunter wears will be dictated by the weather and the type of hunting that is to be done.

Temperatures can be warm to downright hot during early fall hunts. Outer garments of cotton are best for such situations since cotton is light and quiet. Some camouflage clothes in a mottled pattern of green and brown are made of cotton. They can be purchased with shirt and pants separate or as a one-piece suit—either is perfect for bowhunting. Hunters can wear fluorescent orange vests over the camouflage if hunting with firearms. A bright-colored cap or hat is also a good idea for warm-weather gun hunters. Camouflage hats are fine for archers, but if you buy a camo cap with a brim, it may be best to wear the hat backwards so it won't interfere with your draw.

A shirt and pair of pants or jeans can be worn under the camo outfit if it isn't too warm. Long underwear should be considered if you are hunting early mornings and evenings when temperatures are cool, especially when spending most of your time on stand. Still-hunters or drivers probably won't need longjohns until daytime temperatures are consistently cool.

There are three types of long underwear: fishnet, cotton knit, and heavy insulated. I wear knit underwear, but many deer hunters prefer the fishnet weave. It is a matter of personal preference. To see which is most comfortable for you, try them both. Insulated underwear is best for cold-weather use. In extreme cold these are sometimes worn over knit or fishnet underwear.

Always try to dress in layers for deer hunting. Bring along enough garments to keep warm in the coldest weather. If it is warmer than expected, some layers can be shed. Hunters unprepared for cold thermometer readings can't put layers on they don't have.

Tennis shoes with a light pair of socks are fine for still hunting or stalking early in the season. If thorns or cactus are a problem in your area, a light pair of leather boots might be a better choice. Rubber footwear is the ticket for walking in wet terrain. Whenever I wear out a pair of waders, I cut off the heavy boot and wear these deer hunting early in the fall. There are no laces to worry about, they are durable and light. Wool or cotton socks are satisfactory for use in early fall.

Outer garments should be wool for cold-weather deer hunting. This material insulates you from the cold even when wet, and it is quiet. Trackers, still hunters, and drivers who won't be standing in one place long may do fine with a set of longjohns for an inner layer on the bottom. Three layers should be considered for the upper body. A shirt, sweater, or light sweat shirt can be worn over a longjohn top followed by a wool coat or hooded sweatshirt. Wool garments and outer layers of sweat shirts should be bright colored (red or orange is common) when gun hunting. If you are hunting in a state that requires wearing

Felt-liner boots are the warmest the author has found. Tennis shoes are quiet and light for warm weather still-hunting or stalking. Rubber boots are necessary for walking in wet terrain.

Wool clothing is best for cold weather deer hunting. Dressing in layers is also advisable.

orange and your clothes are red, simply wear a fluorescent vest over the sweat shirt or coat and fluorescent hat on your head.

Stand hunters need maximum protection from the cold since they won't be moving. I know because I spend a lot of time on stands in cold weather, sometimes when temperatures dip below zero. My legs are covered with one or two long john bottoms, a pair of jeans, and wool pants. On the upper part of my body I wear a long john top, a shirt, a sweater, one or two sweat shirts, and a heavy coat. I sometimes top off my outfit with a snowmobile suit. The number of layers are varied in accordance with the current weather conditions.

When hunting with bow and arrow in snow I wear a pair of white coveralls for camouflage. The green-brown pattern is worn when no snow is present. All of the outer garments I wear deer hunting are purchased in sizes that permit wearing several layers underneath. If normal-size outer layers are obtained for deer hunting, they will be tight and make it difficult to move comfortably.

I do not wear all of my clothes when walking to a stand. If I did, heavy perspiration would be inevitable and the chances of getting chilled once situated would be increased. A portion of my heavy clothes are carried in a pack until I reach my destination. I try to start heading for a place I want to sit early enough so there is no need to rush.

Something to cover the head is as important as warm clothes when sitting in cold weather. A lot of heat escapes via an uncovered head. I prefer a wool skull cap or short-billed hat, but any type will do that you are comfortable with.

A flap of wool sewn to the back of a cap or hat prevents snow from falling down a deer hunter's neck when the white stuff covers trees. As far as I know, El Harger from Munising, Michigan, originated the idea. The cap modification was explained to me by a friend of his, Andy Tingstad.

Another way to keep snow from falling down your neck is to wear a scarf. Scarves protect the front and back from cold breezes as well as snow.

Don't wear a hood over your head if at all possible. The material covers your ears and dulls your hearing.

Either white coveralls or the typical green-brown pattern will do for camouflage when hunting in snow.

Author prefers a skull cap when hunting in cold weather and often wears a snowmobile suit over other layers when on a stand.

Some deer hunters use suspenders to hold up their pants, but I prefer a belt. I usually carry a sheath knife on it and can use my belt to drag a deer if I forget a rope. A tracking hunter I know wears a belt from six to eight inches longer than normal so he can tuck shed layers of clothes under it when he is moving on a track.

Raingear may be necessary on some deer hunts. Ponchos in yellow or green are fine in many cases. Two-piece outfits will keep hunters dryer than ponchos. Yellow is the brightest color I've seen rain suits in; so an orange vest should be worn over the top of raingear during gun seasons. Wool clothing will keep hunters dry during periods of light rain or in snow.

Boots that come with felt linings are the best I've found for keeping my feet warm in cold weather. I wear the leather-top, rubber-bottom variety. The felt absorbs perspiration. My boots, like my clothes, are purchased at least one size larger than normal to accommodate plenty of socks. I wear from three to five pairs of heavy socks to fill out my boots. After a day of hunting, be sure to remove the felt liners to let them dry.

Rubber or leather boots are okay for deer hunting in situations where you won't be staying in one place long. I like to wear plenty of socks with these boots, too.

Hands need protection during cold weather. I wear light cotton gloves whenever possible. They are not bulky; so I can easily handle a

Andy Tingstad is wearing a cap with a wool flap sewn on the back to prevent snow falling down his neck when deer hunting in snow-covered woods.

gun, bow, or camera with them on. Wool gloves are my second choice. I carry a pair my grandmother knitted for me years ago. When my cotton gloves get wet or the temperature takes a nosedive, I wear these. I sometimes stick gloved hands in my pockets to keep them warm during long waits in cold weather.

Bowhunters who use a three-fingered shooting glove can keep that hand warm by cutting the middle fingers off a cotton glove for that hand. The shooting glove can be strapped on over it.

Proper clothing; a gun, bow, or camera; ammunition or arrows; and a hunting license are the essentials for deer hunters. Before venturing into the field, however, hunters should slip a few additional items in pockets or a small pack. One item no deer hunter should be without is a compass. Don't just buy one, try it out to make sure it is accurate and you know how to use it.

Before going in the woods, mountains, desert, swamps, or whatever, try to take a compass reading to determine which way you are heading in and which way you will have to go to get back out. It only takes a couple of seconds.

Metal from a gun will sometimes throw a compass off; so set your gun down when taking a reading and walk a few steps away from it. When deer hunting it is also a good idea to look at a map or carry one with you that shows all roads, powerlines, railroad tracks, lakes, and streams in the area you will be hunting.

When turned around in areas that have roads or identifiable features on all sides, simply use a compass to head in one direction. You will eventually come out to someplace familiar. If you ever become totally lost in a wild area where the potential for finding familiar ground in one or more directions isn't likely, the best thing to do is stop where you are and build a fire. Wandering aimlessly in wilderness is a waste of energy and will only make matters worse.

To build a fire you will need matches, which are something else every deer hunter should carry with him. Book matches are fine, but carry some in a waterproof case on the chance those in a pocket get wet. Aluminum match cases are available in sporting goods stores. I use spent shotgun shells (plastic) to keep my matches dry. Twelve-gauge and 16-gauge cases fit together snugly. It is a good idea to include a striker with matches in a watertight container.

If caught in a situation where you need to build a fire and matches are in short supply, it is possible to make two matches from one. Simply split either a stick or book match down the middle with a knife. When striking the halves hold a finger near the head for support; otherwise they will bend easily and may not light.

Ponchos are handy to have along on deer hunts when rain is expected.

Deer hunters should always carry a compass with them and know how to use it.

If the woods are wet when you want to start a fire use the inner bark of birch trees, small twigs that grow under dense-needled pine trees, birds nests, or unravel threads from a sweater to use as tinder. The tissue or paper towels you should have with you can also be used to start a fire. Tissue can be used in other ways, too. It comes in handy if nature calls, to blow your nose, or to dry a scope lens. Paper towels can be used to wipe the inside of a dressed deer carcass or your bloody hands after the chore is done. Rubber gloves can be included in your gear if you want to keep hands clean and dry while dressing a deer.

Don't forget a knife to dress a whitetail or muley with. Either pocket or sheath models are fine as long as they are sharp. A stone or kitchen sharpener can be included with your gear if you expect to skin a deer in the field. A folding saw or hatchet is useful to open the pelvic area or quarter a deer.

A plastic bag will be useful for holding the heart and liver from that dressed buck or doe.

You will want to carry a flashlight to help you see before daylight or after dark. I like the two-cell models, but some hunters get by with small penlights. Regardless of the type used, be sure it has fresh batteries. It is a good idea to carry spares, too. If you have a flashlight reserved for use during deer season, try to remember to remove the batteries or turn one backwards after you are done hunting for the year so they won't corrode.

A length of stout rope is another item you don't want to be without. It will be useful to hang or drag a mule or whitetail deer. Thin rope or a piece of wire should be included to fasten a tag to that buck or doe. A ball of string or roll of surveyor's ribbon will be useful to mark your way to or from a stand, the trail of a wounded deer, or the route to take to reach a deer left in the woods overnight.

High-energy snacks such as candy and granola bars, raisins and brownies should be carried while deer hunting. A thermos of coffee, bouillon, or soup can be great pick-me-ups on cold days. Also try to pack a lunch if you plan on being in the field most of the day. If you are operating out of a car or camp, you may want to return to it for lunch. If so, thermos and sandwiches don't have to be carried with you, but try to make it a point to carry candy or raisins with you in the woods. Then you will always have them to fall back on in case something comes up and you don't get out of the woods when expected.

An optional item you might want to carry is a camera. Photos of a bagged buck, scenery, and camp scenes will bring back fond memories in future years. Try to remember to bring a flash unit or flash cubes, too. Many of the best exposures on a deer hunt will be possible in low light situations.

Binoculars or a spotting scope are also optional, but they can be a tremendous aid in any type of deer hunting, especially in open country. Tracking hunters should consider bringing sunglasses to wear since staring at snow for long periods can be hard on eyes.

Bowhunters may want to include a stick of camouflage coloring for application to their shiny, white faces or a hood that pulls down over the face. I prefer stick camo myself. Visibility isn't impaired as it sometimes is with a hood. The face paint washes off without any trouble after a day of hunting.

An arrow sharpener can also come in handy in the field. A file or kitchen knife sharpener will do for a quick touchup on heads that missed their mark.

If the weather is so warm that mosquitoes and biting flies can be ex-

Deer hunters who will be in the field all or most of a day should carry a lunch with them in a day pack. This hunter is wearing an orange vest and hat, which are required for gun hunting in many states.

These are some of the things deer hunters should carry with them. They include high-energy foods such as raisins or candy bars, a lunch, a knife, tissue, a small rope for tag, flagging, camera, waterproof matches with striker contained in empty shotgun shells, a flashlight, plastic bag, a compass, and stout rope for dragging or hanging a deer.

pected, insect repellent should be brought along on a deer hunt. OFF comes in towelettes that fit easily in a pocket. This brand and others are also available in convenient-to-carry small bottles.

Scents used to mask the human odor come in similar bottles. You may want to bring one of these concoctions along on a hunt. I've used scents a few times, but generally don't. I always try to be in a position where deer can't smell me. That is the safest way to avoid detection. There are times, however, when deer appear where they aren't expected. A scent that masks a hunter's odor could be advantageous in such a situation, providing it isn't unnatural. The aroma of apples, for example, is out of place in the mountains, deserts, or deep forests where apples don't grow. Scents that smell like a deer or skunk, on the other hand, will be accepted just about anywhere there are deer.

174

A piece of thread tied on a gun, bow, or at a stand will serve as a constant reminder which way the wind is blowing. The least little breeze activates it. I always have a piece of thread tied to my bow quiver. A strand can be attached to the trigger guard on a gun.

Deer or predator calls can be useful at times while hunting whitetails or mule deer. A blast on them will sometimes stop a running buck long enough for a shot. Deer calls are discussed in chapter 9.

Slingshots often come in handy when hunting brushy draws. Bedded deer can be tricked into showing themselves if you flip a stone into a thicket from an observation point.

All of these items aren't necessary on a deer hunt; however, it is a good idea to get in the habit of carrying some of them for precautionary reasons. These include a compass, waterproof matches, flashlight, and raisins, candy or granola. A rope, knife, flagging, and tissue paper are also basics for the deer hunter. You may not need these things most of

A pair of binoculars can also be useful to deer hunters.

the time, but the one time you do need them and don't have them, you will kick yourself.

A compass is something I seldom use unless hunting unfamiliar country. Even in new territory I often manage to get by without using one. Nonetheless, I always carry one when in the field. One morning I needed it when I least expected I would. I was hunting in familiar country, terrain I could almost say I knew intimately, when I got turned around. The problem was caused by a heavy snow the night before. I simply couldn't get my bearings without my compass because many of the landmarks I normally used to navigate were blotted out by the snow.

Small day packs or fanny packs are excellent for carrying some of the extra gear a deer hunter should have with him. Nylon packs are generally quiet. Bright-colored material is best for a deer hunting pack.

14

Guides

I learned some lessons about how to choose a guide for deer hunting the hard way.

Colorado used to have an early-season rifle hunt in high country wilderness areas primarily for trophy mule deer bucks. The season was in August; so the buck's antlers were still in velvet. Due to the remoteness of the terrain coupled with my lack of experience hunting muleys at the time, I decided to hire a guide and outfitter.

It took me three years and a lot of money to find an outfitter who offered what I wanted. The first one I signed up with took as many hunters as he could fast-talk into booking with him. Consequently, his camp was overcrowded and service was lousy, but he was in a good area.

The second year I had a guide who limited the number of hunters in his camp and was conscientious about care of his clients; however, his approach to finding deer at that time of year wasn't adequate. I can say that now, but didn't know it at the time. The territory he hunted had a low density of deer.

Year number three, everything fell in place. I hired an outfitter who restricted the number of hunters in his camp, knew how to hunt deer extremely well, and was in a good area. The man's name is Rudy Rudibaugh from Parlin, Colorado. He operates the 711 Ranch when he isn't in the high country. I hunted with Rudy for a number of years with both gun and bow and took a nice buck each time. The reason I mention Rudy's name is that truly good guides like him are hard to find.

Guide and outfitter Rudy Rudibaugh (left) poses with one of his hunters, Mike Julian, and nontypical, 18-point buck Julian collected.

If I knew then what I know now, I probably never would have booked with either of the first two outfitters. The first fellow I signed up with offered the cheapest rate of any I contacted. He also guarenteed me a buck with at least four points on a side.

The saying that "you get what you pay for" is as true for guides and outfitters as anything else. Good guides don't come cheap. When a hunter pays for a cheap hunt, that is exactly what he gets. I should have also questioned my bargain-priced guide's guarantee of success. A 100 percent chance of success is unheard of, with the possible exception of hunting preserves or game farms, on any deer hunt I know of that is run on the up-and-up.

After my first experience with an outfitter, I was happy to locate one the second year who told me how many hunters would be on the hunt and leveled with me about my chances of scoring. My mistake this time was not comparing the area this guy operated in with others in the state.

Permits had to be obtained to hunt in his area. The number of permits were limited. Additionally, only bucks with four points on a side were legal. These factors indicated the territory had a limited surplus of deer. The restrictions were imposed to prevent an overharvest.

There were other locations in the state at the time that had healthier deer populations, which were also reflected by hunting regulations. No restrictions were placed on the number of hunters who could try their luck in Rudy's area, for example. And any antlered buck was legal.

The problems I encountered finding a satisfactory guide were my fault. I simply wasn't careful enough in making the selection at first. For that reason I suggest that deer hunters interested in securing a guide or outfitter try to investigate all the angles thoroughly before committing themselves. The only way the selection process can be done properly is to start looking well ahead of a hunt: from six months to a year or longer in many cases.

Advance planning is a must for hunters interested in trying their luck in states such as Wyoming, to make sure licenses are obtained. Applications have to be in well before the season, by March 1, when a drawing is held to fill the quota of nonresident licenses. Hunters have to be assured of getting a license in Wyoming and states like it before securing a guide or outfitter.

Even though a firm committment can't be made to a guide or outfitter in Wyoming, for example, until the hunter knows he will have a license, tentative arrangements should be correlated with deciding on where to hunt because a specific region has to be written in on a license application.

I should point out here that deciding on an area with the highest possible density of whitetails or mule deer in any given state isn't a prerequisite to enjoying a successful guided hunt, although it should be considered. Good guides can usually get their hunters into deer regardless of their abundance because they are familiar with the country and the animals' movements within it.

There are a number of ways to get the names and addresses of reputable guides and outfitters. Some outfitters advertise in the classified sections of outdoor magazines such as *Outdoor Life, Field &*

Mule deer buck taken on guided hunt in Colorado.

Stream, and *Sports Afield.* Some are mentioned in magazine articles, too. Additional listings are carried in The National Rifle Association's hunting annual. State and provincial departments of fish and game plus guide and outfitters associations can also provide contacts. Chambers of commerce are good contacts in Texas, for one, to get a line on deer-hunting services. Addresses of state and provincial agencies that provide information on guides and outfitters can be found in chapter 3.

Word of mouth is another source of information on guiding outfits. Acquaintances who have gone on guided hunts can provide a name or two along with a recommendation or a word of caution.

Here is a list of associations of guides and outfitters with their addresses:

Alaska Professional Hunter's Association, Box 4-1932, Anchorage 99509.

Colorado Guides & Outfitters Association, Inc., Sweetwater Route, Gypsum 81637.

The Outfitters Professional Society, Inc., Box 45, Trappers Lake Route, Meeker, Colorado 81641.

Idaho Outfitters & Guides Association, P.O. Box 95, Boise 83701.

Montana Outfitters and Guides Association, Box 631, Hot Springs 59845; Montana Outfitters & Dude Ranchers, P.O. Box 382, Bozeman 59715; Montana Wilderness Guides Association, Route 6, East Rattlesnake, Missoula 59801.

Professional Guides & Outfitters Association of New Mexico, P.O. Box 455, Albuquerque 87103.

Oregon Guides and Packers, Inc., P.O. Box 132, Sublimity 97385.

Wyoming Outfitters Association, P.O. Box 1365, Cody 82414.

Western Guides and Outfitters Assoc., 1717 Third Ave., #212, Prince George, British Columbia V2L 367.

Northern Ontario Tourist Outfitters Association, Marten River, P0H 1T0.

Quebec Outfitters Association, 2860 Chemin des Quatre Bourgeois, Quebec, G1V 1Y3.

As names and addresses of operators are obtained for the area you want to hunt, write them an introductory letter. Make it as brief as possible. Tell them what type of hunt you are interested in and the weapon you plan to use. Some guides only handle bowhunters or those who use firearms. Also ask for information on their rates, services, past success, and references from recent seasons (names and addresses of hunters who have used their services).

Some guides operate out of comfortable lodges and use vehicles as the principle means of travel to and from hunting areas. Others get into backcountry on horseback and tent out with their hunters. Drop camp arrangements are also possible. In this situation an outfitter provides a fully equipped camp and leaves hunters on their own, then picks them up at a later date. Hunters who have a complete line of camping gear may simply want an outfitter to transport them and their gear to and from a remote campsite.

Some guides or outfitters may be eliminated by their initial response or lack of one. The next step involves corresponding with the references mentioned by operators who reply. If one or two guides look more promising than others, check out their references first.

To increase the chances of replies from an outfitter's past hunters, try to ask for brief answers and provide a stamped, self-addressed envelope. The more convenient it is for them, the more likely they are to provide the desired information. Following is a sample letter that could be sent to references.

Dear Mr. Or Ms. ——:

I am considering a hunt with *(guide's name)* in the future and was given your name as a reference. Any information you can provide about your experience with him as a guide or outfitter would be appreciated. Answers to the questions below will help. A return envelope is enclosed for your convenience. Thank you in advance for your assistance.

When and where did you hunt with the person mentioned above? ___
Were you successful?_____
Size and sex of deer, if successful?_____
Other deer seen? _____ _____
Was the guide easy to get along with?_____
Were services adequate?_____
Which ones weren't, if any?_____
Did he seem to know what he was doing?_____
Would you hunt with him again? _____
Why?_____
Do you know the names and addresses of other people who have hunted with him I can contact? _____
Please list:

_____
_____
_____
_____

Additional Comments:

_____
_____
_____
_____

Sincerely,
(Your Signature)

Be sure to find out what services a guide provides. Here Rudy is skinning a buck author took.

Guide and hunter stop to water horses on a horseback deer hunt. Some guides use vehicles as the prime means of transportation.

Some guides operate out of tent camps; others use motels or lodges as the center of operations.

If replies aren't received from hunters you want input from, try calling them. Some people don't like to fill out questionnaires no matter how simple they may be.

Comments from past hunters should give you a good idea who the best guide or outfitter is. Beware of guides who hesitate to give

184

references, unless it is their first year in business. The final selection shouldn't be made until you find out via another letter or two and maybe a phone call what openings he has for the upcoming season, how many hunters will be along, and what the total cost will be for the type of services he provides. Also, make sure you know exactly what services and equipment he will be providing and what he expects you to bring.

Don't be afraid to ask questions. You are going to be shelling out good money for a hunt. Try to make sure you will be getting what you pay for. On the other hand, don't expect your guide or outfitter to be a slave. Help out with camp chores whenever possible, and don't try to tell him how to run his business.

Be sure to ask if there are any special hunting regulations you should know about. Some states require proof of completion of a hunter safety course even if you have been hunting for years. Others have stringent restrictions on the weapons that are legal.

It won't hurt to ask about what weather can be expected, too; so you will know what type and kinds of clothing to bring.

Once dates for the hunt have been decided on, the guide or outfitter may ask the hunter for a deposit. This is a common practice, but make sure you get a receipt for it. Also find out if it is refundable if something comes up and you can't make the hunt.

A guided hunt can be one of the most pleasurable and successful you will ever go on, but it can also be the worst. The difference is often determined by the amount of screening the hunter does before deciding on a guide or outfitter.

15

After the Kill

Once a deer is down, the hardest part of a hunt is over. At that point the successful deer hunter can turn his or her attention to care of the carcass. Proper handling from the time a whitetail or mule deer is dropped until the meat reaches the freezer will insure a supply of tasty venison for months ahead.

A supply of venison is a bonus of deer hunting that my wife Lucy and I always look forward to. The meat is delicious, high in protein, and provides a welcome change of pace from our normal diet of beef and pork. A deer on the meat pole represents an economic benefit to us. Meals we eat of venison reduce the amount of money we have to spend at the supermarket for domestic meats. Frankly, without venison from the spike buck I downed with a musket last December to carry us through the winter, our budget would have been strained further than we would like to admit.

Some hunters insist on considering the cost of firearms, bows, other equipment and hunting expenses such as gas, guide fees, and plane fares as the price paid for venison. The dollar value per pound of venison can be high in many cases using this rationale, much higher than meats available at the butcher shop.

But I think the money I spend on deer hunting buys me the opportunity to hunt deer, nothing more. I don't have to shoot a deer to get returns on the dollar invested in deer hunting. I buy recreational value, a commodity that is difficult to put a price tag on. Countless times I feel

I have gotten more than my money's worth on a deer hunt even though a deer wasn't collected.

Many people spend money to watch football and basketball games for the recreational value involved in watching the teams play. The price of admission doesn't include a meal, neither should deer hunting. That is why I feel venison is a bonus of any deer hunt rather than an economic benefit.

I can honestly say I haven't had any bad-tasting venison from white-tail or mule deer, regardless of the animal's age, if the carcass was cared for properly. Distasteful meat is often the result of poor handling somewhere along the way from the time it was shot until it was cooked. There is no excuse for either.

Once a deer is down and dead it should be dressed (the viscera removed) as soon as possible. Before starting to dress a deer, your tag should be affixed to the carcass. There is no need to "bleed" a white-tail or mule deer by cutting its throat. Most blood that hasn't drained out of the wound will be in the body cavity and will drain during the cleaning process. A cut in the hide on the underside of the neck is definitely not recommended if you think you may want to have your deer head mounted.

If a deer is on an incline, situate the carcass so the head is uphill.

Penis and testicles on bucks can be removed before opening the body cavity. Simply cut the skin around them and they can be pulled away from the body. To start a cut in the skin around the sex organ, pinch a fold of skin between thumb and forefinger then slice it. Opening the skin this way prevents unnecessary cuts in the meat.

A tube is connected to the penis at the rear. Don't cut it. Pull back testicles and penis with tube attached and lay them on the ground behind the carcass. The tube should be cut only after the bladder is removed, which will be a final step. (Some states require that proof of sex remain intact on a deer carcass. In that case these steps can be eliminated.)

To start the dressing process, make a horizontal cut in the belly area while standing over the deer facing toward its head. This cut doesn't have to be long, about three inches is fine. Try to cut in the center of the belly where there is little or no hair. Keep the knife blade, which should be sharp, level when making the cut, and take it easy. Make short, slicing strokes. Do not stab a knife blade into the belly to start a cut. As obvious as it may sound to most deer hunters, I know some beginners who have done so. The intestines or stomach may be ruptured by stabbing a knife blade into the abdominal cavity, which is not desirable.

One of the first things a hunter should do after getting a deer is to tag it. This successful hunter is punching his tag.

When dressing a deer, its head should be uphill if on an incline.

Several layers of muscle and tissue lie beneath the skin. All have to be cut through to reach the body cavity.

After the cut is completed, insert middle and index fingers of the left hand (if right-handed) under the skin and lift it up and away from the viscera. Now you can start a cut toward the head, working the knife blade between your fingers.

Cut at least as far as the rib cage, further if possible. Most heavy-bladed knives that are sharp will cut through ribs. You can use both hands to hold the knife to cut ribs if necessary. There is nothing that will rupture in the chest area. The ribs can be cut as far as the brisket. If, however, you are considering mounting the head, you should stop cutting when even with the back of the front legs.

A better way to open the body cavity is to make the initial opening just behind the rib cage. With a deer resting on its back, there is a space between skin and internal organs here. Therefore, the chances of accidentally rupturing anything are reduced.

Once an opening is cut, use the middle and index fingers to elevate the skin and guide the knife blade toward the rear. The cut can be extended further forward by going back to the starting point and slicing ribs.

Now that the carcass is open, intestines, stomach, and liver can be rolled out on the ground. Use your knife to cut any tissue connecting this material to the sides or back of the body. Kidneys and fat may remain along the back. These can be easily removed by pulling on them.

There will be a thin, muscular membrane across the body cavity in front of where the stomach was. This is the diaphragm. It should be cut free along the ribs and back.

The heart and lungs can be removed next. They can be pulled out once the windpipe is cut. The windpipe is all the way forward in the chest cavity. It is circular and semirigid.

Next, cut completely around the anus so the lower end of the digestive tract and bladder can be pulled forward and discarded. This step is much easier if the pelvic arch can be split open. An ax or saw works best for this, but a sturdy knife blade can be used if you exert enough pressure.

Here a deer is propped up against a tree to aid in draining.

Whichever method is used to get at the lower digestive tract, make sure all material is removed from the anal passageway so blood from the body cavity can drain through it. A cleared passageway will also speed cooling of the meat.

To keep hands clean while dressing deer, some hunters wear rubber gloves. If hunting in exceptionally cold weather where temperatures are below zero, wearing gloves is a good idea. Bloody hands get cold quickly after field dressing is complete.

If intestinal matter got on any part of the meat as a result of cleaning or from wounds, try to wipe it off with leaves, grass, a clean handkerchief or paper towels. An alternative is to cut away a thin layer of the affected meat.

Some hunters remove the glands on the back legs of deer as well as the entire windpipe. I have found neither practice to be necessary.

Once cleaned out, a carcass can be elevated to help it drain. As examples, it can be propped up against a stump, on bushes, or draped over a log. Most blood can be evacuated by simply lifting the front quarters off the ground.

Be sure to salvage the liver and heart from your deer. They are great eating. If you don't want them, it probably won't be hard to find someone who will be willing to take them off your hands. The tongue and kidneys of deer can also be eaten. Carry these items in a plastic bag.

Some hunters prepare and eat the liver from a deer they have bagged the same day. I do the same thing with the tenderloins. They are narrow strips of delicious meat on either side of the backbone. Each one is about a foot long. I usually wait until I get home to cut these delectable pieces of meat out. They can be pulled out once an end has been freed with a knife blade.

Ideally, a whitetail or mule deer should be skinned and butchered the same day it is shot. This is a must when hunting in warm weather, but isn't as critical when temperatures are in the 30 to 40 degree range. Some hunters recommend aging deer carcasses. This is difficult to do properly, except under controlled conditions. I have found that venison tastes better when butchered as soon as possible.

When a deer carcass won't be processed promptly, it should be hung so it will cool. It can be hung with the head up or down. A deer that isn't drained should be suspended head up. If the whitetail or mule deer will be caped, hanging it with the head down is best.

I sometimes hang my deer from a tree in the woods if getting it to camp or home isn't convenient right away. This isn't possible where there are no trees, of course. In such a situation prop the body cavity

If it isn't possible to get a deer out of the woods right away, it should be hung so it will cool.

A deer that is to be caped should be hung head down *(photo credit: Montana Dept. of Fish & Game).*

open with a stick, then roll the carcass over so it rests on its chest, and spread the legs. The carcass should be in shade if possible. Body heat won't be able to radiate properly from a carcass lying on its side; consequently, the meat in the area that is on the ground could spoil if left for any length of time.

If a deer must be left outside in warm weather, flies can be kept away from the meat by sprinkling pepper over the inside of the carcass and on any exposed flesh. Flies will lay eggs on unprotected areas otherwise.

Coyotes and bears won't often bother a deer carcass left in the woods that has been handled by men. A shirt, coat, or some other article hung nearby will help discourage them. If human thieves are a problem in your area, you might try marking the carcass somehow by notching the ears. Or try putting a business card, slip of paper with your name on it, or some other identifying article in the mouth of a dead deer. If your tag is on a whitetail or mule deer, that should be proof enough who the animal belongs to. The local sheriff or conserva-

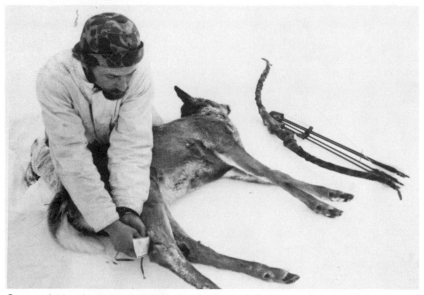

Successful bowhunter attaches his tag to gambrel. To hang a deer head down, a pole should be put through the gambrels on both hind legs.

tion officer should be notified of the theft of a deer and what to look for in identifying the carcass.

There are a number of ways to get a deer out of the woods. Probably the most commonly used method is dragging. This is the best way if there is snow on the ground or there isn't far to go on hard-packed ground. Bucks come complete with handles (antlers) that can be held on to for dragging. If there is a hunter for each side and there isn't far to go, this approach works fine.

A better method for dragging either bucks or does is to use a rope. The animal's front legs should be folded on top of its head then a rope should be tied around the neck and legs. The rope can be tied at an end or the middle. If the middle of the rope is secured around the deer's neck there will be two pieces, one each for a pair of draggers. If there is only one dragger, each of the two pieces of rope can be tied to a stick to rig a makeshift harness.

When the end of a rope is tied to a deer for dragging, it can be adapted to allow two hunters to pull by attaching a sturdy stick or pole to the loose end. The pole should be long enough to extend across the pullers' chests and work like a yoke. When pulling alone, a short stick can be tied to the rope to serve as a handle. This is easier on the hand than gripping the rope.

If for some reason you don't have a rope, a belt will do to drag a deer.

If at all possible, get help to drag a deer rather than do it yourself. Hauling 100 pounds of dead weight, whether on bare ground or snow, is strenuous. It is bad enough with two people, let alone one. Make it a point to take frequent breaks when dragging a deer, even if there are two of you. There shouldn't be any rush to reach camp or the nearest road. Overexertion can quickly turn a successful hunt into a tragedy. More than one deer hunter has suffered a heart attack while trying to muscle a carcass to car or camp.

If darkness is approaching and you want to get out of the woods, hang the deer where it is and go back for it in the morning. But make sure you will be able to find it. Hang a bright-colored coat or vest in a prominent position near the carcass and mark a trail to a road if you are

Antlers are handy handles for dragging bucks short distances.

in unfamiliar territory. Blaze marks can be cut in trees, tissue or surveyor's tape hung on branches, or feet scuffed along the ground to mark the route.

Deer shouldn't be dragged over sand or mud, nor should they be dragged for long distances. If they are, there is a good chance the meat will get dirty and bruised. Alternatives to dragging a carcass are carrying it yourself or transporting it by horseback, boat, canoe, motorcycle, or snowmobile. There are restrictions on the use of motorized vehicles in some states during firearms deer seasons. Be sure to check before using a motorcycle or snowmobile to retrieve a deer.

I have saved myself some long hauls with deer carcasses by dragging them to a nearby river and retrieving them with a canoe. Deer should be carried in a boat or canoe whenever possible, but when there isn't enough room they can be pulled in the water. The carcass will float just below the surface. Hairs on a deer's hide are hollow and will hold the carcass up. If this is attempted on a river, try to go downstream since the submerged deer creates a lot of drag. The inside of a carcass that is

Yoke arrangement for dragging a deer with a rope.

Handle arrangement for dragging a deer with a rope.

194

This pair of hunters have strap for pulling tied to deer at its middle so each has a piece to pull.

dragged in the water should be wiped out thoroughly once your destination is reached. This will remove dirt and speed drying.

I have carried a few deer on my back, and it isn't as bad as it may sound. The best way to do it is to cut the carcass in pieces, either halves or quarters. If a deer is small it can be carried whole, but for safety reasons this isn't recommended during firearms seasons. It can be done safely during archery hunts though. Just the same, a brightly-colored vest or garment should be attached to the carcass.

If you are interested in having the hide tanned or the head mounted, the deer should be skinned before it is cut up. One of the biggest mistakes deer hunters make when caping a deer head that is to be mounted is not allowing for enough hide. It is better to give the taxidermist too much than not enough.

To cape a deer, make a cut through the hide that extends completely around the body behind both front legs. The skin can then be sliced around the front legs where they join the body. A second major cut should be made perpendicular to the first, in the middle of the back. The incision should extend up the back of the neck to a point just below the base of the antlers, providing the deer is a buck.

From there a short slice can be made to the base of each antler. On antlerless deer, make the cut up the back of the neck to a point just past the ears. With these cuts made, the hide can be peeled forward.

The best place to start separating skin from flesh is on the deer's

195

Canoes or boats provide an easy means of transporting deer to camp or car when water is available.

back at the intersection of the two major cuts. Once started with a knife, the skin often peels away from the carcass by pulling on it. After the cape has been skinned as far as the base of the neck, turn your attention to skinning the rest of the hide. You want to leave the cape attached at this time to protect the front quarters from dirt.

The only cuts necessary to complete skinning are on the inside of the hind legs. Once these are completed, the skin can be worked free on the legs and the remainder of the carcass, one side at a time. Skin remaining on the front legs will have to be removed, too. Skin the legs only to the first joint. The lower portions can be cut off after the first joint.

To skin a deer that isn't to be caped, simply extend the cut that was made to dress the animal to the head at the throat. Make the cut up the middle of the chest and the underside of the neck. Then slice the hide up the inside of each leg from the incision running the length of the deer's body. The hide can then be slowly separated from the carcass, working on one side at a time.

The skinning process is more awkward when a carcass is lying on the ground rather than hanging, but it isn't difficult if taken a step at a time. The operation is easy with two people working together.

The carcass can be quartered and the head removed after the hide is separated from it. This should be done while the carcass is lying on the skin. A saw will be necessary to separate the quarters. To quarter a

196

deer, cut the carcass in half across the backbone, then separate the front and rear portions in half again by sawing down the middle of the backbone.

The quartered meat should be covered with the hide or cloth meat bags to protect it while it is carried. A bright coat or vest should be draped over the deer head and hide.

Pack frames are best suited for carrying a quartered deer. The meat can be tied to frames with rope. It is a good idea to distribute the load between two hunters, especially if the deer was big. Each can take half. If alone, two trips may be necessary to transport a large deer.

Hunters who don't care about saving their hide or cape can half or quarter their deer with the hide in tact. Skinning can be taken care of later.

Deer that are to be transported by vehicle can be tied on the car top, over the trunk, or put in the bed of a pickup or in a trunk. Don't put a deer over the hood where heat from the engine will increase the chances of spoilage. If the weather is consistently warmer than 40 degrees fahrenheit and you will be on the road for several hours, use dry ice to keep the meat cool. Quarter the carcass before leaving on a long drive. Then put a chunk of ice between the front and rear quarters and cover them with blankets or canvas for insulation. Ice will have to be replenished on long drives.

Some states require that deer be transported visibly and in one piece. Here again, try to be familiar with the regulations in the state you are hunting.

If a deer wasn't skinned and caped in the field, it must be done at camp or home. A carcass that is hanging is easier to work with. For caping, a deer should be hung upside down. To remove the hide, the carcass can be hung either way.

A stout branch or piece of wood should be inserted through the gambrels of both hind legs to suspend a deer with its head down. Gambrels are on the back of the legs just above the joint. There is an area of skin here between a heavy tendon and the leg bone. This skin can be cut to allow a stick to pass through. Be careful not to cut the tendon.

While the deer is held in position—with the hind legs straddling a beam, pole, or limb—the stick can be passed through the gambrels so it rests on a support. To hang a deer with the head up, a rope can be used to fasten the carcass to a support.

Slice the hide in the same fashion as mentioned earlier for either caping or skinning once a whitetail or mule deer is hung. The hide can often be peeled off the carcass by pulling downward. A knife will be necessary to start the skinning, however. The underside of the tail should be split so the tail bone can be removed.

A head or hide that is to be preserved should be taken to a taxidermist as soon as possible. If more than a day (a few hours if the weather is warm) will elapse from the time a cape or hide is removed from the carcass until it can be delivered to him, salting the hide will be necessary. Before a cape is salted it should be removed from the head by completing the skinning. The best way to do this is to invert the hide over the skull.

Cut the ears off close to the skull. A dull instrument, either a spoon or a screwdriver, is best for prying the skin loose from around the base

Tanned deer hides make attractive decorations.

of antlers. A pair of pliers can also be used to pull hide from the base of the antlers, but take it easy to avoid tearing the hide. Extreme care should be exercised when the eyes are reached. Use a sharp knife to cut the skin flush with the eye socket. The tear duct is on the forward side of the eye. Be sure to continue separating the skin as close to the skull as possible in this area. Caution is required in skinning the nose and lips, too.

The ears must be skinned after the cape is removed from the head. Slowly and carefully invert the skin on the back of each ear over the inner cartilage until you reach the tip.

Before the completely skinned cape and hide are salted, remove any fat or flesh that is clinging to the skin. There is usually a thick layer of meat around the lips. Try to trim as much of this as possible without damaging the skin. Ordinary table salt is fine for applying to capes and hides. Don't be stingy; pour lots of salt on and rub it in all over with special attention to lips, nose, ears, tail, and edges of the hide.

If it will be several days or more before the article is taken to a taxidermist, it should be frozen. Never send a deer hide through the mail enclosed in a plastic bag. After the salted skin dries put it in a paper bag or gunny sack, then wrap it for mailing.

The antlers from your deer must be brought to a taxidermist along with the salted cape. Since he won't need the skull, the antlers can be sawed from it. Start sawing on the back of the skull so the saw blade will pass just below the tops of the eye sockets and complete the cut on the bridge of the nose.

Hunters who shoot a buck with a set of antlers they want to save don't have to go through the expense of having the entire head mounted. The antlers and skull plate can be mounted on a plaque with a piece of felt covering the exposed bone. Antlers mounted this way make attractive decorations. Kits are available with the necessary materials for mounting.

The meat from a deer, like the hide, should be processed as soon as possible. It may be best to care for the venison first if there is a chance of spoilage. I always bring my skinned deer to a local butcher. He cuts the carcass while I wait. Any odds and ends are ground into hamburger. At home, my wife and I package and label the venison, then put it in the freezer. All hair and fat is removed from the meat and damaged portions trimmed as we wrap it.

The process takes time, but proves to be worth it when we enjoy delicious meals of venison in future months. If venison is frozen with the fat intact, the quality of the meat will deteriorate. Removal of fat cuts down on freezer space necessary to store a deer. If freezer space is extremely tight, debone the cuts as well.

The price my butcher charges for his service is so reasonable it would be ridiculous to cut a deer myself. He is an exception. Most establishments that regularly butcher deer charge high fees. For this reason, among others, hunters should know how to cut up their deer. The procedure is simple.

You will need a good meat saw and a sharp knife or two. A work bench or covered kitchen table will do to work on. Use freezer paper or aluminum foil to cover a table, not newspaper. The carcass must be quartered for butchering.

Each of the front quarters can be broken down into six major pieces, then individual cuts can be made from them. First, separate the leg and shoulder from the rest of the quarter. This section can be cut away with a knife by slicing between the shoulder blade and the body. The leg and shoulder can be divided into three roasts. Some people prefer to trim meat from the leg and use it for stews or hamburger.

The neck can be cut next. Meat from the neck is used for roasts, stews, or hamburger.

To divide the remainder of the front quarter further, saw it in half lengthwise and divide each piece in half again. The meaty shoulder area can be cut into roasts or steak. Stew meat, hamburger, or roasts can be obtained from the upper and lower ribs. The brisket is best suited for stewing.

Steaks, chops, and roasts are the primary cuts from the hind quarters, with the exception of the flank and shank. The flank is a thin muscle in the belly area and the shank is the lower portion of the hind leg. Meat from these locations can be used for stews or hamburger.

The loin is a tubular piece of meat that runs along the backbone. This can be cut out and sliced into chops. From that point everything else can be cut into steaks or roasts. To reduce the remainder of the hind quarters to pieces that are easy to work with, cut the back or loin section in front of the rump and make a diagonal cut across the remaining large portion.

Only use your saw on bones; cut any meat necessary to reach the bone with a knife. Hair and fat should be removed from cuts before they are packaged. If freezer space is critical, it is a good idea to debone your venison. Use freezer paper or aluminum foil to wrap the meat. A felt-tipped pen can be used to write the type of meat, the cut, and the date on freezer paper. Make labels out of masking tape when venison is stored in aluminum foil.

Butchering a deer may seem like an endless task the first time it is attempted. This is only because the steps are unfamiliar. The chore will become less tedious in future attempts as you become more proficient at butchering and realize the dividends of your labor will be delicious meals of venison. It helps to have at least two people working together on a carcass. If at all possible, have someone who has butchered a deer before show you how.

The procedure I have listed here for butchering deer is by no means the only way it can be done. Many hunters develop their own routine for reducing a carcass into the cuts they like.

Try to be conservative when discarding bloodied meat that looks like it is beyond salvage. Saltwater is great for getting blood out of meat. Cuts that look bad may be able to be saved by soaking them overnight in a solution of saltwater in a refrigerator.

Many hunters have beef suet mixed with ground venison. My wife and I seldom do this. We use it in things like spaghetti, meatloaf, and casseroles, and it tastes great. Another option for ground venison is to have it made into sausage. Some meat processing plants regularly convert venison to sausage for hunters.

16

Antlers

Antlers are important to most deer hunters. They are symbolic in many ways, but primarily serve as mementos of successful hunts.

Large sets of antlers are accorded special recognition. Those that meet certain standards are listed in one of two record books, depending on what type of weapon was used to bag the deer that wore them. The Boone and Crockett record book lists outstanding racks taken with firearms. Pope and Young classifies record deer heads collected by bowhunters.

Many hunters share the desire to shoot a deer with a record rack, but few succeed in doing so. Whitetail and mule deer wearing antlers that meet record book standards are hard to come by because they simply are not abundant. Those that do exist usually spend their time in remote, lightly hunted terrain.

Numerous trophy bucks are bagged each year. The definition of what a "trophy buck" is varies from one hunter to another. The first buck I shot was a trophy to me at the time and it only had spikes. Now, it would take whitetail and mule deer bucks bigger than those I have hanging on my living room wall to be classified as trophies. My best whitetail has eight points and an inside spread of about 19 inches. The muley has nine points with a spread comparable to the whitetail. Neither is exceptional; many larger racks have been taken, but I am happy with mine.

Something unique about my mule deer head is that the antlers are in velvet. I shot this particular buck during a special early hunt in Colo-

Author's trophy mule deer head.

rado while hunting with outfitter Rudy Rudibaugh from Parlin. Ken Asbury was my guide.

There are two popular methods of classifying the number of points on a set of antlers: Eastern and Western count. In some parts of the West the brow tine or eye guard isn't considered a point, and only the side with the most tines is specified. Take my mounted mule deer as an example. One antler has three points, and the other four discounting the brow tines. That buck would be a four-point by Western count.

Every tine over an inch in length is considered a point by Eastern count. In my opinion this system is best. It coincides with the classification used by Boone and Crockett and Pope and Young. The other method can be confusing because it doesn't give a total picture of what a rack looks like. A four-point buck by Western count can have four points on one side and two, three, or four on the other. The rack may have eye guards or it may not.

It is usually possible to get an accurate idea how a set of antlers is proportioned by Eastern count. An eight-point normally has four on a side; a seven-point generally has four on one side and three on the other. Occasionally a buck will have an odd rack with two points on one side and four on the other, but not often.

On the chance a deer hunter shoots a buck with a rack that might qualify for Boone and Crockett or Pope and Young, he should know how to measure the antlers to see if they will qualify. The procedure is relatively simple. All that is required to score a set of antlers is a quarter-inch, flexible steel tape for measuring (any tape would do for rough measurements) and a piece of paper and a pencil to jot down figures.

Both whitetail and mule deer racks are classified into two categories: typical and nontypical. As you might guess, most sets of antlers fall into the first classification. Typical racks exhibit tines branching from the top of the main beams in an orderly fashion; although there may be one, or several, abnormal points.

There is a slight difference between typical whitetail and mule deer racks. Whitetails have unbranched tines. Points on mule deer antlers beyond the brow tine normally fork.

Nontypical sets of antlers are characterized by numerous points sprouting at odd angles from the main beam and tines, in addition to normal points. Racks of this sort commonly have 20 points or more. Incidentally, for any projection to be considered a point the distance it extends upward or outward must exceed the length of its base in addition to being at least an inch long.

The steps in measuring whitetail or muley antlers for record classification, regardless of the category, are similar. Let's take a typical whitetail rack to start with.

To keep track of figures in an orderly fashion allow for three columns, from top to bottom, on a sheet of paper. Two are for figures obtained from each antler, and the third is for differences in measurements from one antler to the other. Any discrepancies between sides will detract from the total score. Symmetry is an important characteristic of record-book heads.

There is one measurement required for scoring that won't fit into any of the three columns; inside spread of the main beams. It can simply be written to the side or at the bottom of the paper and added in with other figures later.

The first lengths we want to measure are the main beams. These are taken from the lowest outside edge of the burr (circular formation at the base of the antlers where they join the skull) over the outer curve of

This is how to measure beam length, although the actual measurements might have to be done in stages to prevent kinks in the tape.

Length of tines is measured along outside edge.

the antlers to the tip of the main beam. The tape measure should follow the center line of the antler.

It may be necessary to obtain this figure in stages since most beams are curved. A control point should be marked each time a change in direction of the tape is required. All figures should be to the nearest eighth of an inch.

Enter the measurement for the right antler in the appropriate column and the same for the left. If one beam is longer than the other, enter the difference in the third column. (See sample score sheet for further guidance.)

Now, measure the length of each normal point on each antler. The tape should extend from the nearest edge of the main beam to the tip over the outer curve of the tine, to arrive at an accurate score. Tips of main beams are not measured as points. These are considered in the figure for the antler lengths.

Measurements of corresponding points on each antler are then compared and any difference is written in the appropriate location. Typically, a record whitetail buck will have from eight to 14 normal points; however, a greater number is possible.

Circumference of beams at four points is next. The first one is gauged at the smallest point between the burr and first tine. Jockeying the tape around in that area may be necessary to locate the smallest circumference. The smallest circumference between the first and second points is considered next, followed by a like position between second and third and third and fourth. In cases where the first point or brow tine is missing, the first two circumferences can be taken at the smallest point between the burr and second point.

The next step is tallying the total length of abnormal points. These should be measured from their base, whether on the main beam or a tine, to the tip along the outside curve. On a typical whitetail head any points that jut out at odd angles from the main beam or branch from any of the tines are abnormal.

Occasionally, a point coming off the top of the beams may be considered abnormal. Let's look at an example. Say one antler has six points and its mate seven. The extra tine is between the second and third points and is only four inches long. Point number three on the opposite antler is 10 inches long.

If the four-inch tine were considered normal, it would become the third point and scored with its longer counterpart. This way six credits would be lost, and there would be no mate for the fifth point on the side with the most tines and additional credits would be lost. So consider that extra point abnormal. Only four points would be lost that way.

Sample Score Sheet for Rough Scoring Deer Heads

Example: Typical Whitetail

	Column 1	Column 2	Column 3
	Right Antler	Left Antler	Difference
1. Length Main Beam	$23^2/_8$	$22^7/_8$	$^5/_8$
2. Length First Point	$5^6/_8$	$5^6/_8$	—
3. Length Second Point	$7^1/_8$	$7^3/_8$	$^2/_8$
4. Length Third Point	9	$8^7/_8$	$^1/_8$
5. Length Fourth Point	$8^6/_8$	$8^5/_8$	$^1/_8$
6. Length Fifth Point			
7. Length Sixth Point			
8. Circumference between Burr and Second Point	$5^3/_8$	$5^3/_8$	—
9. Circumference between First and Second Point	$4^7/_8$	$4^6/_8$	$^1/_8$
10. Circumference between Second and Third Points	5	$4^7/_8$	$^1/_8$
11. Circumference between Third and Fourth Points	$4^6/_8$	$4^7/_8$	$^1/_8$
12. Total lengths of Abnormal Points (on typical heads this figure is subtracted from score, but is added to nontypical tally)			$3^2/_8$

Inside Spread of Antlers: $21^1/_8$

Total Column 1:	$73^7/_8$
Total Column 2:	$73^3/_8$
Spread Credits:	$21^1/_8$
	$168^3/_8$
Column 3:	$4^6/_8$
Total Score:	$163^5/_8$

Final score for this head is $6^3/_8$ points short of the minimum qualifying tally (170) for a typical whitetail in the Boone and Crockett Record Book. However, it would easily surpass the minimum for Pope and Young (125).

Enter the figure obtained from abnormal points in column three.

The final measurement that affects the score of a rack is the inside spread of the antlers. This must be assessed at right angles to the center line of the skull and can be taken at the widest point between beams.

If the figure obtained is greater than the longest main beam, the difference must be entered in column three on the tally sheet. A number less than or equal to length of the longest main beam can be written in as credit for inside spread.

For instance, let's say the inside spread of the head on the sample score sheet came out to be an even 25 inches, instead of $21^1/_8$. In that case it would be greater than the longest main beam, which was $23^2/_8$. So their difference, $1^6/_8$, would go in column three and spread credit would be $23^2/_8$.

An official scorer for Boone and Crockett or Pope and Young will jot down several additional measurements that simply indicate the conformation of the rack. They don't affect the score. These are the number of points on each antler, tip to tip spread and the greatest outside spread.

Once all of the necessary measurements are determined the final score can be totaled. To tally this figure add all the numbers in columns one and two plus the inside spread. Then subtract the total of column three from that total.

Minimum qualifying score for a typical whitetail rack in Boone and Crockett is 170. Pope and Young accepts scores of 125 or higher.

If a rack is close to or surpasses these minimums, it should be taken to an official scorer for verification. However, 60 days must have elapsed from the time the head was collected until it is officially measured. This allows for drying, during which time some shrinkage occurs.

During early hunts in some states deer antlers may be in velvet when collected. Velvet must be removed from the rack of an animal taken in this condition that is to be measured for record book consideration.

The same procedure as above can be followed for scoring a nontypical whitetail rack. However, the total length of abnormal points is added to the score rather than subtracted. Tally of abnormal points should be listed as a plus figure along with inside spread, rather than placing it in column three as before.

Minimum score for nontypical whitetails taken with firearms is 195,150 for bow and arrow.

The guidelines for measuring and scoring mule deer racks is nearly the same as the technique for whitetails, with a couple of minor exceptions. Muleys usually have fewer normal points than whitetails, often

Circumferences are measured at several locations.

Length of abnormal points is added to the score of nontypical heads, but subtracted from typical racks.

four per beam, not including the beam tip. There is no limit to the number of normal points that may be present.

Due to the difference in structure of muley racks, circumferences must be taken accordingly. As with whitetails, the first two circumferences are measured between the burr and first point and the first and second. The third one, however, is gauged between the main beam and tine number three. The final circumference is assessed between the second and fourth points, always at the smallest place.

Minimum Boone and Crockett scores for typical and nontypical muleys are 195 and 240. For Pope and Young qualification they must be 145 and 160.

A list of official Boone and Crockett scorers in your area and other information can be obtained by writing to: North American Big Game Awards Program, c/o Hunting Activities Department, National Rifle Association of America, 1600 Rhode Island Ave., N.W., Washington, D.C. 20036. Pope and Young information can be obtained from Scott

Here is how to tape inside spread of rack.

The buck that grew these antlers at 2½-4½ years of age obviously didn't have the genes for growing a big rack.

M. Showalter, Box 1001, Garden City, Kansas 67846; or Naomi J. Torrey, Route 1, Box 147, Salmon, Idaho 83467. The departments of natural resources and fish and game in each state might also be sources for determining who official scorers are in your area.

Photos of a trophy head, front and sides, plus a $20 registration fee must be sent with official score charts that are to be considered for record book entry.

Deer antlers are not true horns. Unlike antlers, horns such as those worn by sheep and pronghorn antelope are not shed, although an outer sheath is on pronghorns. Deer shed their headgear every year. Most antlered whitetails and muleys are bucks, but occasionally a doe will sprout a set.

Bucks normally drop their antlers early in the winter, after the rut is over. Both beams may be lost at approximately the same time, or there could be a week or more lag from the time one antler is lost until its mate drops off. The timing varies from deer to deer. All of the bucks in a given area won't lose their racks at the same time either. The health and age of individual animals makes a difference. Severity of the weather is also thought to affect the length of time deer hold their antlers.

In my home state of Michigan, bucks start dropping antlers toward the latter part of December. Yet, a few will be seen still wearing headgear as late as March. In Florida, buck's antlers are reportedly lost and grown with no pattern due to the relative consistency of the weather.

Circular patches of raw skin called pedicels are visible on a buck's head for a day or two after his rack is shed. They heal quickly. A new set of antlers starts to sprout in the spring, by late April or early May in my part of the country. The growth rate of antlers is tremendous, especially on large-racked deer. Their development is complete by August, which is late summer in the northern states.

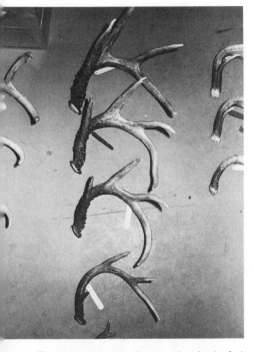

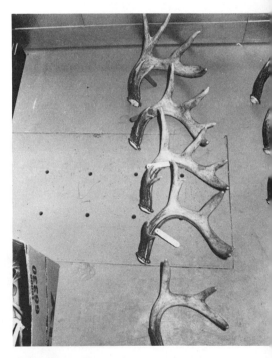

The buck that grew these antlers had a fork as a yearling, but each year after that, 2½-5½, the antlers carried the same number of points and had the same general structure. The only major change was an increase in beam circumference.

These five antlers were grown by a buck when 3½ through 7½, from bottom to top. A forked brow tine was grown from age 4½ on. Second tine also forked at age 7½.

While the antlers are growing they are covered with what is called velvet or moss. It is true skin. All of the tissue is soft and generously supplied with blood during the development stage. If the delicate antlers are damaged or the deer itself injured while they are growing, one or both sides of the rack can become malformed. This is how some nontypical antlers result. Bucks with hormonal imbalance or permanently damaged sex organs may produce nontypical formations year after year.

Once antlers are completely developed the supply of blood to them stops and the tissue dies. Then the velvet is rubbed off, leaving hardened antlers. Coloration of antlers varies from bleached white to a deep brown. My theory is a buck that lives in open country where his antlers get a lot of exposure to the sun will generally have a lighter-

In the presence of many mature bucks this yearling grew sublegal antlers despite the fact he had plenty of high-quality food.

colored rack than a buck that spends most of his time in heavy cover where the sun seldom penetrates.

Some sources claim that antlers are stained by dried blood when the velvet is shed. Others feel that antlers derive their color from the trees they are rubbed on when polished. A combination of these factors may play a role in antler coloration.

The size rack a buck grows is dependent upon three factors: heredity (genetics), nutrition, and age. Deer that grow outstanding headgear have to be in good health, at least several years old, and genetically disposed to antler growth. Even yearling bucks can have respectable heads sporting eight or more points, providing their diet and parentage is right. Yet, some bucks can be healthy and old, but sport a mediocre rack because the right genes aren't there.

Interestingly enough, a buck's antlers will form in the same general pattern year after year. The number of points may increase the first couple of years, but the general shape and features of the rack will normally remain the same.

John Ozoga, a wildlife biologist with the Michigan Department of Natural Resources, showed me several series of antlers shed by the same bucks over a period of years. The deer were in an enclosure and could be monitored closely. The resemblance of the racks from one year to the next for each animal was remarkable. In many cases the only change over a span of years was an increase in the circumference of beams. John could identify individual bucks during his observations by the shape of their racks.

Another fact the biologist learned from his studies of penned deer is that antler growth in yearling bucks can be adversely affected by an abundance of older, mature bucks. In situations where big-racked bucks were common, a percentage of the yearlings in the population grew sublegal antlers, less than three inches in length. Food wasn't a limiting factor here since the deer were on a high-nutrition diet.

17

Deer Management

Strictly from a management point of view, it would be better if either whitetail and mule deer bucks didn't grow antlers or both sexes did.

An adequate harvest of antlerless deer (does and young-of-the-year bucks) is difficult to achieve in parts of the United States due to a stigma many deer hunters today have grown up with against shooting deer that aren't wearing antlers. If both sexes of deer did or didn't have antlers, the problem wouldn't exist.

I believe part of the reason a percentage of deer hunters resist harvesting does is because of their poor understanding of deer management. Since it will be easier to try to get hunters to understand and accept the need for shooting both bucks and does than developing a strain of antlered does or antlerless bucks (maybe), let's get on with it.

It would be nice if deer herds could continually increase by simply protecting does, but unfortunately, that isn't how things work. Each chunk of deer range only has enough browse to feed a certain number of deer throughout the year. Available deer food is lowest during the winter; so the maximum number of whitetails or muleys that can be supported in any given habitat without reducing its quality (its carrying capacity) is determined by the amount of food available to them then. In many cases the winter deer range is only a fraction of the size of the summer and fall range. Muleys and some whitetails have traditional wintering areas, which they use year after year. Their nutritional needs must be met within that limited area.

The key to a healthy deer herd is maintaining its winter level at or below the carrying capacity of its habitat. A herd that comes through the winter in good shape will produce a maximum yield of fawns. By fawning time deer will have distributed themselves throughout the summer range where there is an abundance of food, enough to sustain the increased population. Before winter returns, the number of whitetail and mule deer in an area has to be trimmed back to correspond with the limited food supply.

That is where hunting comes in. The purpose of the fall hunting season is to reduce the population to the level the winter range can sustain. To do this, the number of deer that were produced for the year (as close to it as possible) must be shot. Both bucks and does can and should be harvested to reach that goal.

After all, both sexes were fawned. More of each sex than were reproduced would have to be removed from the population before there would be a net decline. Looking at it another way, some does can be shot and the herd will still increase if fewer are harvested than were produced for the year.

The number of births and deaths in a deer population have to balance out with the food supply. Imagine a platform balanced on a central pivot point like a teeter-totter. Births and deaths are on each end and food is in the center as the balancing factor. The scale may tip one way or another for a time, but will eventually return to a balance.

If a deer herd is well below the carrying capacity of its range, allowing the animals to increase is good management. This can be done by protecting does entirely for a time or harvesting a fraction of those produced each year. Does can't be protected indefinitely though if that route is chosen. An increasing population will reach its limit, then must be maintained at or below that level. To do that the annual increase, which is made up of both bucks and does, must be removed each year. A herd at a level that is below the capacity of its habitat is preferable to one at the limit. It is like having money in the bank.

Populations of whitetails or muleys that have gone beyond the carrying capacity of their range are the biggest problem in deer management. In order to bring them back in balance, more deer have to be removed than are produced each year. Many times it is difficult to achieve a large enough kill.

Overpopulations reduce the habitat's ability to sustain deer. More deer food is consumed than is produced. Some food sources are killed off entirely with overuse. The number of deer their habitat will be able to support in future years will decline for each year the herd stays above capacity.

If hunters are unable or unwilling to reduce a deer herd on a year-to-

Ground hemlock is a preferred deer food. When deer overpopulate they reduce this to . . .

. . . this. With proper management, situations such as this can be avoided.

year basis, the health of the population suffers. In stress situations created by extremes in weather, such as winter, some of the excess whitetails or mule deer will die of malnutrition. Those in weakened condition will be easy prey for predators.

The worst side effect of an overpopulation of deer, one that few hunters are aware of, is their reduced capability to reproduce.

A biologist said it better than I can, "Reproduction is a luxury. That animal (doe deer) is geared for its own survival. If there isn't enough food, deer just won't reproduce. A doe may become pregnant, but the young will be aborted or some other means will be used to get rid of it."

In such a situation, too many does are usually the problem. A doe left to live under these circumstances can be a detriment rather than an advantage. Many fawns born to weakened does will be dead at birth or die shortly afterward. Some of the young will live, but only a fraction of those that would have survived if the herd were healthy.

As odd as it may sound, more fawns will be produced by fewer does in a healthy condition than twice as many winter-weakened females. Research has shown that on properly managed deer range 30 percent of six-month-old does will produce a fawn, 90 percent of the yearlings will fawn (some with one and others with twins), and adult does will usually produce two.

In contrast, adult does on poor range will average from .4 to 1 fawn each. Younger does in such a situation are nonproductive.

Simply looking at figures from adult does, the advantages of maintaining a healthy range and deer herd become apparent. Ten healthy does can be expected to have 20 fawns. Twenty poorly nourished does will reproduce a maximum of 20 young.

Going one step further using the same reasoning, deer hunters can harvest more whitetails and muleys annually from a properly managed herd than from one that is out of balance with its habitat, even though there are fewer animals carried through the winter in the first instance.

Sounds simple on paper doesn't it? It is, really. But how do deer managers know what the carrying capacity of habitat is, how many deer are using it, and how many of each sex should be harvested?

In the field there is no way to account accurately for every deer. However, their numbers can be estimated reasonably accurately. This is done in a variety of ways. One method consists of counting groups of deer pellets on randomly chosen plots. It sounds far out, and maybe a bit ridiculous at first, but think about it for a minute. When scouting for deer one of the signs hunters look for is droppings. The frequency with which they appear provides a rough index to what extent the area is being used.

When done scientifically, the number of pellet groups in an area actually does represent the number of deer in an area. Biologists know through studies how many times a deer defecates in a day. This information combined with random sampling and statistical probabilities and calculations provides a reasonably accurate estimate of populations. The entire procedure is too sophisticated to detail here, but it has proved to be one of the best ways to determine deer numbers.

There are other methods of estimating deer populations such as marking individuals, aerial surveys and others. Each is based on sound information and involves complex mathematical computations. The important thing to keep in mind about deer population estimates is they allow for error. Figures reflect upper and lower limits rather than a single, cut-and-dried number, even though they may be listed that way.

As an example, the deer population of a two-square-mile wintering area near where I live was recently estimated. Researchers concluded that from 361 to 543 deer wintered in the yard. The same thing is done for individual management units and entire states.

The carrying capacity of an area is determined in a fashion similar to the way some deer population estimates are conducted. Random plots are chosen, then edible browse is cut and weighed. Mathematical computations are used to complete the survey. It is important to realize that when estimating the amount of browse that will be available in wintering areas, only the material that will be within reach of whitetails and muleys is considered. Much of the food hunters see in the fall will be covered with snow in winter or is too high for deer to reach.

Population and browse estimates are used to determine how many deer of each sex can be harvested. The number of hunters expected and harvests achieved in previous years are also considered. Additional variables deer managers try to take into account are deer losses to poachers, predators, and automobiles. Another important consideration in Western states is competition between livestock and deer for available food supplies.

States are usually broken down into a number of different management units because of varying conditions often present within each. Harvest goals are normally determined for each unit.

It is seldom a problem to get a desired harvest of bucks. To encourage the take of antlerless deer, hunters are sometimes offered them as a bonus to the regular limit. Some areas have a two-deer limit and one of the animals must be antlerless. Others offer camp or party permits that can only be filled with a doe or young-of-the-year buck.

Another option is hunter-choice permits. A hunter holding one can shoot either a buck or doe. Additional possibilities exist and are in use.

Some years the hunt goes as expected and an appropriate number of deer are harvested. There are others, however, when not enough or too many whitetails and mule deer are bagged. Variable hunting conditions and hunter densities may make animals more or less vulnerable than expected. The deer range is surveyed every year to keep tabs on its status. Part or all of the deer killed each season are examined as well to determine their physical condition. If wintering areas are overutilized more deer will have to be removed from the population the next season through liberalized regulations.

Malnourished deer in the winter are a sure sign of too many animals. Biologists can determine the condition of dead deer by breaking open a bone on a hind leg and looking at the bone marrow. A healthy animal will have white, tallowy marrow from the fat contained in it. Malnourished deer will have exhausted much of the fat in bone marrow, leaving it red and gelatinous.

Underutilized wintering areas usually result in restrictive hunting regulations to allow herds on such range to increase.

Habitat changes and reduction are also major considerations in deer management. Even though a herd is maintained at or below the carrying capacity of a particular range, its capacity to support as many deer as it formerly did may be reduced as the vegetative growth, usually trees, matures. Forested areas with numerous openings, both grassy and logged types, are ideal for deer. Habitat such as this will support a maximum number of deer. As trees crowd into grassy fields and they grow up out of reach of deer, the habitat's deer-supporting capability is reduced. The same thing happens when habitat is flooded or developed in some way that makes it no longer useful to deer.

When the habitat is lost the whitetail or mule deer that formerly occupied it have to move to other areas or, if there isn't room elsewhere, they will be removed from the population, preferably by hunting. Remember, the birth-and-death rate of a deer population has to balance out with the food supply.

Habitat that is maturing is not a lost cause in many cases. It can be brought back to maximum deer production and maintained there through manipulation or improvement. Logging is one of the best ways to keep a necessary portion of deer range young. Controlled burns, natural fires, and herbicide use also improve living conditions for deer.

When logging is utilized to improve habitat, trees should be cut every five to 10 years. Obviously, this can't be done to the same group of trees that often. Most take much longer than that to mature. The

Logging is one of the best ways to maintain and improve deer habitat in forested areas.

practice that is used to manage forests, both for deer and timber production, involves keeping as much of the habitat in mixed-age stands of trees as possible.

In an ideal situation a percentage of the trees in an area will mature at five- to ten-year intervals. For example, consider a 40-acre stand of 40-year-old aspen. It can be cut on a 40-year cycle. A 10-acre clearcut could be made every 10 years. By the time the last 10 acres were cleared, trees on the first area that was cut would be mature again. When done on larger acreages a continual patchwork of openings can be maintained.

This illustrates how habitat management works. It would be great if all deer range was suitable for such a scheme. There is so much diversity, however, that individual management plans have to be developed for each range. Unfortunately, a large percentage of deer habitat across the U.S., much of which is privately owned, isn't managed at all. State lands suitable for deer production are usually managed under the guidance of foresters and wildlife biologists with the departments of fish and game or natural resources departments.

Deer hunters who own land that isn't currently managed may be able to improve the habitat and realize an increase in deer on their property, which would result in better hunting. State game biologists, foresters, and county extension agents are usually available to help develop a suitable management plan. Private landowners can realize financial benefit from timber sales for habitat improvement as well as increased deer numbers.

A way to increase benefits of cutting to deer is to cut in the winter when natural browse is scarcest. Felled treetops represent tons of nutritious food to whitetail and mule deer. This is a form of feeding deer, but it is beneficial, unlike the artificial feeding of corn, hay, and pelletized food that is practiced in some areas.

Artificial feeding does more harm than good. First of all, the digestive systems of many deer cannot handle a rapid change in diet. Bacteria are present in their stomachs to aid in the digestive process. The type of bacteria varies, depending on the type of food that is being eaten. Deer that have been feeding on woody material, for example, cannot adequately utilize corn or hay given them when there is a shortage of natural food. In the case of corn, kernels that are eaten by hungry animals lay undigested in the rumen where they ferment and form a poisionous gas, ammonia, that may kill them.

This problem does not exist when whitetails or muleys feed on tops of trees, their natural food.

Deer can use artificial food adequately during the winter when fed these rations throughout the season. Their digestive systems will adjust to it. This type of artificial feeding builds an artificial herd, if done on a continuing basis. Deer numbers will go higher and higher and the quantity of food necessary to feed them will increase steadily, as will the bill for food.

While the herd is building, their winter habitat will deteriorate. Its capacity to provide natural browse will reach low levels. Although the artificially fed deer herd that has overpopulated its winter range may not need the browse, they will eat whatever is available.

Eventually, a point will be reached when not enough artificial food can be provided. The inevitable then happens: deer die. If rations are drastically reduced or eliminated, a major decline in the population occurs. Liberalized hunting regulations are necessary to harvest the number of deer required to avoid great death tolls under these circumstances.

Live-trapping the animals would be too costly and impractical in most situations.

The only way an excessive build-up of deer can be avoided in an artificial feeding situation is to crop off the annual production every year. Sound familiar? This practice is the same as maintaining a herd within the carrying capacity of its natural food supply. Artificial feeding

221

simply is not necessary if the habitat is healthy and the deer population using it is in balance with the natural food supply. If there are too many deer in an area, removing the excess number or improving the habitat to accommodate them are better alternatives than artificial feeding.

An artificial deer-feeding situation that proved to be a problem existed in a national park in upper Michigan: Pictured Rocks National Lake Shore. The affected area is known as Beaver Basin. Deer that wintered in the basin were artificially fed for years while it was privately owned by the Michigan-Wisconsin Pipeline Company. The company spent thousands of dollars every year to sustain the whitetails.

The herd was well in excess of the carrying capacity of its range when the Park Service acquired the land. They have a policy against artificial feeding of any wildlife. Rather than halt feeding altogether, rations were reduced while a special hunt was planned to thin the herd. Some local residents opposed the hunt because they felt estimates of the herd size were too high and there was enough natural browse to sustain it in the winter. As a result, no special hunt was held and the herd died off more than a hundred per season. This was with supplemental feeding. There would have been a dramatic crash had the feeding been stopped entirely.

Hundreds of deer that could have been harvested by hunters died. In the process the habitat was damaged further. Because of this, it will take more years for that wintering area to rejuvenate to the point a herd of any size can be maintained than if hunters had removed the surplus. If the hunters who opposed the hunt had a better understanding of deer management, those animals could have been put to better use than as food for predators and other scavengers.

As an offshoot of poor deer or habitat management, predators are often wrongly blamed for declines in deer populations. In Beaver Basin, for example, a number of deer were killed by coyotes and bobcats, a higher number than would have been susceptible if the herd were healthy. Winter-weakened deer that may die anyway are easy prey for predators.

Loss of fawns is often attributed to predators, too. In reality, many does on poor range simply don't produce living fawns.

Such predators as coyotes, bobcats, wolves, and mountain lions certainly kill deer, both young and adults, from healthy populations. Their kills, however, are usually not responsible for the decline of a population any more than hunter kills are. As mentioned previously, deer managers take predation into account when setting harvest goals for hunting seasons. As long as total deer mortality is the same or less than

Deer managers take the number of animals killed on highways into account when setting hunting regulations.

reproduction for any given year, the population will not decline. In my opinion, predators have as much right to deer as hunters do. They certainly earn their kills. If human hunters were as skillful as predators at getting close to deer, there would be no need for this book.

Before leaving the subject of predators, I would like to add that their populations may, at times, reach higher levels than desirable. When they overpopulate they also have an adverse impact on their food supply. For this reason, predators must be managed, too, but they don't deserve the reputations and treatment they have gotten from many deer hunters who would like to eliminate them entirely.

One of the biggest barriers to blanket acceptance of deer management decisions is getting hunters to accept the validity of population figures. They spend hours in the field and many of them see few whitetail or mule deer. This leads them to believe there are few animals around, unless they are able to see plenty of tracks, droppings, or other deer sign. Anyway, the next season when wildlife biologists say there is an overabundance of deer out there and more does have to be harvested, the hunter becomes skeptical.

223

There are two primary reasons for opposing assessments of deer numbers. Some hunters spend each season, year after year, in the same area. They come to accept the territory they are familiar with as representative of their region, if not their state. Actually, there can be tremendous differences in deer densities in areas separated by 50 miles or less. Most states are divided into management units to compensate for these differences, but it isn't always possible to separate accurately all units. Major roadways are often used as boundaries. These seldom coincide with differing deer herd considerations.

The second major reason for differing opinions on deer abundance is that many hunters give themselves too much credit and deer too little. They expect that if there are a lot of deer in the area they will see a lot, if there are only a few they will see a few. It works this way sometimes, but not usually. Both whitetails and muleys are geniuses in avoiding hunters. And many hunters aren't as keen at sneaking through the woods or picking a stand as they think they are. I have been skunked while deer hunting enough times myself when there were plenty of deer around to realize a hunter's limitations.

To substantiate my last point I will leave you with some facts and figures from a couple of closely monitored hunts in Michigan. One took place on a five-square-mile island in Lake Michigan—South Fox Island—during 1970. At that time the population of deer on the island was estimated to number approximately 600 animals. That meant there were about 120 deer per square mile!

The bag limit was three deer, two of which had to be antlerless. There were a total of 612 hunters who took part. They bagged 382 animals. Only 1 percent of the hunters collected three deer, 14 percent got two and 31 percent took one. A whopping 54 percent of the hunters were unsuccessful; some of them didn't even see a deer during their hunt!

The second closely monitored Michigan hunt was held inside a one-square-mile enclosure with a known population of deer. There were 39 of them: 7 bucks, 14 does and 18 fawns. Seven experienced deer hunters hunted in the enclosure for four days. A total of eight deer were taken—three does, four fawns and one buck. Only one of the seven bucks was sighted during the course of the hunt!

Hunts were held in the enclosure for seven years. The results each time proved that hunters are inefficient, only sighting a fraction of the population present in an area. This study was conducted in an area of limited size. On larger tracts of land hunters probably see an even smaller percentage of the actual number of deer present.

18

Bonus Seasons

All I could see was a group of bobbing antlers heading toward my brother and me. Six mule deer bucks were taking their time, feeding as they came. There were two bucks with big racks in the bunch. The one in the lead looked the best; so I riveted my attention on him.

When the lead animal was 150 yards out and still coming, I put the crosshairs on his shoulder, uncertain about waiting any longer to take him.

Bruce's reassuring words were what I needed: "Let him come. Take your time."

When the buck was between 100 and 125 yards away he turned to our right and was broadside. I figured that was the closest he would get. The buck jumped straight up in the air when my 150-grain .30-06 slug connected; then he took off running. A second hit put him down for keeps. The mule deer's rack had five points on a side.

Another time when I was hunting whitetails with a muzzle-loader there were a pair of young bucks working toward me across an opening that had been recently logged. One had spikes, and the second had a small rack with four points. When the bigger-antlered buck was still about 80 yards away it looked like he scented me; so I decided to try a shot.

I aimed for his shoulder and touched the trigger on my .50 caliber Hawken made by Thompson/Center Arms. The breeze whisked the smoke from the shot away quickly enough for me to see the buck bounding away with its tail wagging—a sure sign of a miss.

I took this muley buck on early hunt in Colorado.

Something happened next that I probably will never experience again. Three magnificent bucks, each with racks carrying at least eight points, appeared one after the other from a lane to my left and trotted by me only 35 yards away! They continued by me into a swamp. I simply stood there and watched them disappear, almost not believing what I saw.

There wasn't enough time to reload the musket. Even if there would have been, I couldn't have shot anyway. I felt sure my round ball missed the buck I shot at because of his actions, but I couldn't be positive until I checked.

My reason for recounting these deer hunting experiences is because they both occurred during bonus seasons. They were special hunts designed to increase the harvest of an underutilized segment of the deer population or to increase recreational opportunities for deer hunters.

I collected the mule deer in Colorado during late August. The buck's antlers were still in velvet. The early-season rifle hunt was only held in certain high-country wilderness areas that were often inaccessible to hunters because of snow during the state's regular deer season. As a result, bucks that reside in these mountainous retreats were underharvested. An early season provided better harvesting of these deer and an excellent opportunity for hunters to collect trophy bucks.

Incidentally, this bonus season hasn't been held in Colorado in recent years in order to allow the deer herd to increase. The early hunt may be revived in the future.

That unusual concentration of whitetail bucks crossed my path on a December hunt in Michigan after the close of the regular firearms season. The late season was established to give muzzle-loading deer hunters a bonus opportunity to collect a buck if they were unsuccessful in filling their regular firearms deer tag. The added time afield is a boon to hunters and does not adversely affect the deer herd. It is difficult to overharvest bucks during a primitive weapons hunt.

The best time to hunt deer is whenever you can, but bonus hunts such as those I've described often provide a better opportunity to see whitetails or mule deer and bag one than regular seasons do. Sometimes pre- or post-season hunts simply offer deer hunters additional time to fill one license, as is the case with Michigan's black-powder hunt. It all depends on the circumstances. Other times deer taken during bonus seasons won't affect hunters' regular season bag limits.

After missing a bigger-antlered buck I downed this spike during late season musket hunt.

This is usually true in cases where an area has an overpopulation problem or an extra incentive is required to get hunters to participate. An example of such a situation is South Fox Island, which is part of Michigan and lies in Lake Michigan. Because it is remote (20-odd miles out in the lake), it is difficult to attract enough hunters there every year to harvest enough deer to prevent overutilization of the habitat. Deer tagged there with bow or rifle don't count on a hunter's regular license. Post-season hunts were held on the island for a couple of years, but now the season there coincides with dates of deer hunts on the mainland.

A change in weapons may be all that is necessary to take advantage of bonus deer hunting seasons in many cases. As I've already mentioned, switching from a modern rifle to a musket will give hunters added time afield in Michigan. The same is true in other states. Hunting with bow and arrow in addition to firearms often opens the door to additional deer hunting opportunities. Most states have separate seasons for archers and firearms hunters. Archery hunts usually precede those for firearms users, but some are also held afterward. A few states restrict deer hunters to the use of only one weapon a year; so be sure to check local regulations.

My only regret about bow hunting for deer is that I didn't start sooner. The first years I hunted deer were with firearms exclusively. Then I started bow hunting. I wasn't as successful in bagging deer with a bow as I had been with a rifle, at least at the outset. More important though, I saw more deer than I had ever seen before, had plenty of opportunities to score, and learned a lot more about deer. The pleasant weather common during bow seasons added additional appeal to bow hunting for deer.

In the long run, I became a better firearms hunter because of what I learned while bow hunting and a better bowhunter because of my experience hunting whitetails and mule deer with rifles and shotguns.

Early fall bonus seasons are often rewarding because deer densities are at the highest levels possible. In addition, whitetails or muleys that haven't been hunted since the previous fall won't be extremely wary. It is not unusual to see bucks traveling together, especially muleys, at this time of year.

The only drawback to some early deer hunts is they are sometimes held in remote areas with rough terrain, which makes the territory hard to reach and the hunt a physical challenge. I was hunting between 10 thousand and 12 thousand feet above sea level in the Rocky Mountains when I downed the mule deer mentioned earlier. The going was tough, but the beauty of the surroundings at that time of year made the hunt

Hunting with bow and arrow as well as firearms makes additional hunting time available to deer hunters.

Late hunts are a good time to collect big bucks.

worthwhile. The weather was pleasant for the most part on the mountain hunt, but temperatures commonly fell below freezing at night. Rain was almost an everyday occurrence, too, and snow fell occasionally.

The weather during late season deer hunts can be downright miserable, but this is one factor that increases the vulnerability of whitetail and mule deer to hunters. Thermometer readings were below zero the day during muzzle-loader season when I saw five bucks in a matter of seconds. Temperatures were the same throughout the hunt. All of those deer were feeding on the tops of trees that had been felled by loggers.

Cold weather had the deer moving and feeding. Bucks were feeding especially heavy during this period. The rut was over, and they were trying to regain some of the weight lost during their preoccupation with breeding activities.

Deer are sometimes more accessible to hunters in larger numbers during post-season hunts, too. Mule deer characteristically move to lower elevations with the approach of winter. Some whitetails also move to wintering areas, "yards."

This movement concentrates large numbers of deer in smaller areas than they occupied earlier in the fall and makes animals easier to find.

Late hunts are a great time to collect big bucks. Deepening snow usually forces them out of inaccessible haunts to areas where hunters have more chance to see them. Despite the fact that deer may be concentrated and feeding more during late seasons, they can be difficult to bag. The animals are often super-wary because of earlier hunts.

Bonus deer seasons that are held on a statewide basis are usually open to an unlimited number of hunters. The number of participants are normally regulated under a permit system when special deer hunts are held in limited areas. Permits are often allocated during a random drawing from the selection of applicants or on an first-come-first-served basis.

An advantage of bonus deer seasons, whether early or late, is light hunting pressure, even in situations where participation is not limited. While the odds of seeing other hunters is low during special hunts, the opportunity to get a look at deer may be better than any other time of the year. At the very least, these seasons provide extra hunting time. For what more could a deer hunter ask?

19

Sportsmanship
and Hunting Ethics

Ethics, sportsmanship and safety have always been important in deer hunting, and will continue to be. In recent years and in the future, however, they have had and will have a new emphasis. They will not only be determining factors for the quality of each individual's hunting experience, but also who, if anyone, will hunt.

There are people who don't understand or approve of hunting. They not only don't hunt themselves, but also many of them don't want anyone to do so. These individuals are organized in an effort to stop, or at the very least, restrict hunting. Examples of unethical unsportsmanlike, unsafe behavior provide them with ammunition that can be used against hunters and hunting. Any and every incident that may portray hunting or hunters in a bad light are seized and amplified, sometimes distorted.

A television special on hunting labeled as a documentary and called "The Guns of Autumn" is a perfect example of this technique. It was aired in September 1975. Many, if not all, of the sequences in the show were atypical of hunting as most of us know it. Some of the scenes and sound effects were allegedly changed, according to hunters who took part in the filming. Anyone not familiar with hunting could have easily accepted "The Guns of Autumn" as a fair representation of the pursuit and formed opinions against it.

The Michigan United Conservation Clubs (MUCC) currently has a $300 million damage suit filed against CBS for the show. MUCC contends that portions of " 'The Guns of Autumn' malign all hunters through deliberate distortions." Co-plaintiffs in the suit are Thomas L. Washington, MUCC executive director; Fred Bear, internationally known bowhunter; Ben East, a noted outdoor writer on the staff of *Outdoor Life* magazine; State Representative Thomas Anderson of Southgate, chairman of the House Conservation Committee; and Carl T. Johnson of Cadillac, a member of the Michigan Natural Resources Commission.

There have been lengthy delays in court on the suit; so the proceedings have not made any noteworthy progress. It will probably be years before the case is settled.

A similar case revolving around a television program titled "Say Good-bye" developed in the early 1970's. Alaska sportsmen were involved in this suit. Film of a polar bear tagging project was changed to make it look like hunters illegally killed a sow with cubs from a helicopter. The case was settled out of court in favor of hunters, according to lawyer John Hendrickson of Anchorage, who represented sportsmen.

If there weren't any instances of behavior or actions that are derogatory to hunting, antihunters wouldn't have gotten as much attention as they have. Unfortunately, unethical and unsportsmanlike hunters do exist. In a way, the antihunting movement has been beneficial in bringing attention to undesirable hunters and hunting practices. Once these have been identified something can be done about them. If we as hunters fail to correct any problems that exist, there may come a time when none of us will be able to hunt. To clean house, so to speak, it will be necessary to insist that unethical and unsportsmanlike hunters are kept out of the field.

There was a time when each hunter was held accountable for only his actions. This is no longer the case. Every action of any deer hunter reflects on all deer hunters. How I represent myself as a hunter in the field, and anywhere else for that matter, has an impact on you as a deer hunter, and your conduct, likewise, will affect me. For this reason, each deer hunter has a responsibility to all other deer hunters to behave in an ethical, sportsmanlike, safe manner.

What qualities does it take to be an ethical hunter, a safe hunter, a sportsman? Are the qualifications tough to meet?

The guidelines are so simple, such common sense things, that every hunter should easily be able to meet them. Before going into them I want to point out something that should be obvious: all three qualities are interrelated, although they are not necessarily the same. It is difficult to possess one without the others, but it can be done. Generally, an ethical hunter is a safe hunter and a safe hunter is usually a sportsman, and so on.

My dictionary defines ethics as the "basic principles of right action." A sportsman is described as "one who abides by a code of fair play." Some people label anyone who hunts a sportsman. To my way of thinking that is the way it should be, but at this time I would consider it a misuse of the word. Safety is "the state or condition of freedom from danger or risk."

The way I read the definitions, sportsmanship is determined by following the rules and regulations of hunting, which in most cases are laws. An ethical hunter does what is right in a hunting situation even though he or she may not be specifically bound by law to do so. It isn't always possible, however, to draw a line between the two.

Consider this example. On my first mule deer hunt I spotted a huge-bodied deer while still-hunting that was no more than 50 yards away, with its head hidden behind an evergreen tree. Only bucks were legal. The shoulder area of the animal was visible; so I could have shot the deer. In all probability, due to the animal's size, it was a buck.

I didn't shoot though. In fact, I didn't even consider it. I waited until the deer, which indeed was a buck, a huge-racked one, showed himself before attempting a shot. As it happened, the muley finally detected my presence and came in the open on the bounce. I missed.

When I told my story to the other hunters in camp one of them said, "Why didn't you shoot him when you had an easy shot. If it had been a doe, no one would have known the difference." That man, whom I wouldn't have been sharing a camp with if there was a choice, was totally wrong. I would have known the difference if I shot a deer without identifying the sex and it turned out to be a doe.

I can thank my father as the first among many who instilled attitudes in me becoming of a sportsman and ethical hunter.

Anyway, if I would have shot that buck when I first saw him, even though I didn't know it was a buck at the time, I wouldn't have broken the law. Shooting before I saw antlers would have been wrong, however, because the possibility of breaking the law existed. So was what the other hunter suggested unsportsmanlike or unethical? In my opinion it was both.

There are times when, according to the definitions, ethical and sportsmanlike behavior can be separated. Suppose a freshly wounded deer comes by your stand. You have a moral and ethical obligation to finish that animal if possible, although you may not be required by law to do so.

The same considerations apply if the hunter who wounded the buck or doe comes on its track. You killed the deer, you can tag it. At least offering the whitetail or muley to the person who drew first blood would be the right thing to do, depending upon the severity of the wound.

Deer hunters have an ethical responsibility to their quarry to: first, use an adequate weapon and projectile that can be handled efficiently; second, try for a clean killing shot; third, expend every effort possible to trail and finish a wounded animal; and fourth, clean and care for the meat properly.

One year my brother and I helped another party of hunters track a whitetail one of their members wounded. It proved to be a two-day effort to kill the doe. I dropped the deer, but relinquished it to the other hunters, as we planned to do from the start.

Hunters also have an ethical obligation to each other and hunting to pick up litter left by others; to avoid unnecessary public display of dead deer; to understand deer management practices; to avoid unnecessary conversation about the kill, dwelling more on the many other aspects of deer hunting such as sights, sounds, and feelings that are seen, heard and experienced during days in the field.

I think it is extremely important that hunters be more conscious of what they say about hunting. I have heard tales from well-intentioned hunters that almost turned my stomach. Imagine how a nonhunter (not necessarily an antihunter) would take such accounts. Stories from hunters themselves may easily convert a nonhunter to an antihunter.

Something I have done a lot of thinking about is the classification of hunting as a sport. In the truest sense of the word I don't think hunting is a sport, but rather a sporting endeavor or pursuit. A sport is usually thought of as a match or contest between two willing teams or players that provides recreation. There is no doubt that hunting provides plenty of recreation. Take the word willing out and hunting fits the rest of the definition, too.

"Willing" is the key word though, at least from the antihunters' point of view. Deer certainly don't participate in a hunt willingly. Calling hunting a sport can be and has been criticized for that reason.

No one can argue that hunting as it is practiced today is not a sporting endeavor. Regulations in most cases are designed to give deer more of an advantage than they already have over hunters by restricting the time and manner in which a hunter can harvest them. Many hunters handicap themselves further by using bows and arrows, muskets, and handguns in their pursuit of deer.

My line of reasoning here may be classified as nit-picking by some individuals, but I think it has merit.

To be sportsmen, deer hunters should hunt only during prescribed hours, not take more whitetails or mule deer than specified by law or those of a protected sex, not shoot protected species of wildlife, ask permission before hunting private land, not litter (spent cartridges are litter), and make sure of their target before shooting, which leads us to safety.

As I mentioned earlier, sportsmen are usually safe hunters. Most hunting accidents then, are caused by gun or bowhunters who are acting in an unsportsmanlike manner. Carelessness also enters the picture in many instances.

I remember reading an account several years ago in which carelessness and breaking a game law proved to be a deadly combination on a deer hunt. A pair of hunters were working through some heavy cover when one of them spotted a grouse in a tree. Grouse season was closed, high-powered rifles shouldn't be shot in the air, and the fellow didn't know where his partner was. He shot anyway. The bullet killed his companion.

This is only one example of many. Another illegal trick that often results in hunters ending up on the wrong end of their guns is carrying them loaded either in a vehicle or in camp. Leaning a firearm that is loaded against a tree, a building, or on a car is asking for trouble, too. Poor gun handling also accounts for its share of woundings and deaths. Shooting down a road, resting the barrel of a gun on an occupied boot, and disregard for which way the muzzle of a gun is pointing are a few examples.

A firearm should always be treated as if it is loaded. Whenever picking one up check to see that the chamber is empty, don't take someone's word for it. After a day in the field make sure all shells are removed from magazine and chamber. Work the action over and over again; then look or feel in the head of the chamber and magazine to insure no unejected shells remain. Don't remove only the cartridges you thought you put in. Sometimes, somehow there happens to be one more than there was supposed to be.

I will never forget an experience that taught me a lesson in this respect. When returning to my car after hunting I used to remove the number of shells I *knew* I put in, then point the firearm at the ground, away from the vehicle or anyone with me, and pull the trigger so the gun wouldn't be stored in a cocked position. One evening when I did that, my gun discharged. There was no real harm done, except the unexpected shot scared me. That lesson taught me to check and double-check to make sure all ammunition is ejected.

To illustrate that my experience wasn't a freak, a similar incident that happened to a friend of mine is worth mentioning. On his way home from deer hunting my friend was stopped by a conservation officer who asked to see his gun. He assured the officer the rifle was unloaded, which he was sure it was, but when the warden worked the action a cartridge came out.

Never point a gun or an arrow in the direction of people or buildings. Always know where hunting partners are. If there is a chance they are in the line of fire of a deer, don't shoot. No whitetail or mule deer is worth the possible injury or death of a person.

Horseplay and guns don't mix. Neither does alcohol and hunting. Always try to make sure there are no obstructions in the barrel of a gun, only use the proper ammunition, always keep the safety on until ready to shoot and never shoot at a flat, hard surface or water.

If crossing a fence or some other obstruction pass the rifle, shotgun or bow over or under first. Break the action or unload it if it is necessary to carry it. Use a rope to lift and lower unloaded firearms and bows to and from tree stands. Also try to use safety belts when in a tree stand to prevent accidental falls.

Above all else, be sure of your target. Seeing a movement, a color, or hearing a sound is not enough to warrant a shot. Also as a point of safety, firearms hunters should not wear garments of brown, black, or white. Many states now require gun hunters to wear fluorescent orange in varying amounts, which has significantly reduced mistaken-identity accidents. It is a good idea to wear garments of this material even if it is not mandatory.

One other point: just because a deer hunter happens to be carrying a gun in the woods doesn't mean it must be shot. Firing at tin cans and various other inanimate targets will only spook deer the other way. Target practice should be done on the range.

Bowhunters must be extremely careful with broadheads. If they are as sharp as they should be, they are capable of causing injury at any time, not just when released from a bow. Keep heads in covered quivers until ready for use. Never shoot a broadhead up in the air.

Many states now require young hunters to pass safety courses before they can obtain a license. This is an excellent way to make sure future generations of hunters will be adequately versed on safe hunting practices. When young hunters are starting out is the best time to get them thinking of safety.

Our father saw to it that my brother and I completed a hunter's

Tree stand hunters should use a rope to lift their weapons to them once in position. In the case of a bow, as shown here, it can be hung on a limb, then retrieved when in position.

safety course before we got our first hunting licenses. He also emphasized safety when in the field with us. From my experience I can appreciate the value of early introduction to gun and bow safety.

Each deer hunter should not only strive to be ethical, safe, and a sportsman, but he or she should also expect the same from hunting companions. This becomes especially important for safety. It is a

237

proven fact that the vast majority of hunting accidents involve members of the same party.

One of the best ways to become acquainted with sportsmen in your area is to join a sportsmans club. Another benefit from membership is most clubs have facilities for target practice. Membership in sportsmans clubs on the local, state, and national level is also a great way to promote proper hunting practices and get the hunter's story to nonhunters.

National Hunting and Fishing Day, which is now an annual observance, is one of the best ways to do this. There are ways to tell your story on a continuing basis, too. One club in California, for instance, collects outdoor magazines from its members for distribution in school libraries, doctors' offices, and other key locations where they are sure to be read. Another way to reach people is through club-sponsored slide shows and lectures at schools or meetings of civic organizations. Deer and deer hunting are popular topics. Many groups are interested in learning more about both.

A sportsmans club near where I live makes sure everyone entering and leaving the city gets a reminder about safety and sportsmanship in hunting. There is a sign along the highway that carries a message on each side. One side reads, "Stretch Your Story, Not Your Bag Limit," and the other, "Recognize Your Game First, Then Shoot." They are simple reminders, but passing motorists think about them. Drawing attention to these qualities is sure to help the image of the club as well as hunters in general.

Sportsmans groups should also be constantly vigilant for newspaper articles or letters to the editor that make hunters look bad. Try to respond to them in a sensible manner in a letter to the editor. If facts have been twisted, do your best to straighten them out. Most people read their local newspaper; so this is an excellent way to reach nonhunters.

Clubs can display their disapproval of the shooting of protected animals or birds by offering rewards for information leading to the conviction of guilty parties. This helps the legitimate hunters' image.

One winter some poachers using bows and arrows got into a local deer pen that was part of a small zoo, killing three of the animals. Our archery club immediately reacted by offering a reward to help in locating the culprits. We let everyone know our disapproval through radio broadcasts and letters in the local paper.

The criminals were not apprehended, but at least the public was made aware serious bowhunters weren't going to take the blame for such actions.

Reminders such as these help the hunter's image, plus make them more conscious of their responsibility.

The New Mexico Bowhunter Association has got an even better idea. They have a standing offer of a $50 reward for information leading to the arrest and conviction of any bowhunter who breaks game laws. Their offer is printed in the state's annual big game hunting pamphlet. Another New Mexico sportsmans association in Doña Ana County uses the same means to advertise a similar reward.

Illegal hunting activity is probably one of deer hunting's biggest black eyes. Estimates in some states put the illegal deer kill as high or higher than the annual legal kill. Always try to be on the watch for poaching or other infractions of game laws and report any incidents to local officials. Some states have toll-free numbers hunters can call to report violators if an officer can't be reached. The Michigan United Conservation Clubs sponsors a poacher-patrol program. Under the program tipsters turn in poachers anonymously and can claim a reward by using an identifying number.

Before concluding this chapter I would like to point out that a hunter's attitude toward hunting and the game pursued probably has the most bearing on whether or not he will be ethical and exhibit sportsmanship.

Hunters who view hunting primarily as killing, for example, and feel they must get a deer at all costs, can't be ethical or sportsmanlike. They often must break game laws to attain their goal. These individuals miss out on the true benefits of hunting.

Hunting's primary benefit is recreational: simply to be in the outdoors; to relax in space unconfined by walls and buildings; to see, hear, experience, and learn about the many aspects of nature. Learning about deer, respecting deer, is a major part of deer hunting; shooting a deer is of minor significance. Nonetheless, all of us want to be successful in our attempts to bag a deer, even though the odds are against most of us. Realizing all of this is part of the attitude that breeds ethics and sportsmanship. You try your hardest against the odds, savor every moment afield and hunger for every clue that will tell you something about a particular whitetail, muley, or deer in general so that you *might* see one, *might* kill one.

Yet, when the season comes to a close and you haven't scored, you feel satisfied that you tried your best and can accept hunting for what it is: hours, days, months, and years of looking, learning, waiting, searching, and hoping—not killing. It is enough to whet a true deer hunter's appetite for the next season.

20

Success without Success

Features of my surroundings were losing their distinctness, as they always do toward dark at the end of a day of deer hunting. This time it was more than the end of a day, however, it was the end of a season; and I hadn't gotten a deer.

Actually, my attempts to bag a deer spanned three seasons: there had been a regular firearms hunt, the special muzzle-loading season, and a period for bow and arrow. These were the final minutes of that last season. My chances of getting a deer for the year faded with the light.

I climbed down from my tree stand and walked to a nearby road to wait for my partner to pick me up. I would be lying if I said I wasn't disappointed. I was. After all, anticipation of connecting with a deer was one of the primary motivating forces responsible for getting me in the woods in the first place. There was more behind my being in the outdoors day after day though.

The disappointment wasn't solely because I didn't get a deer. The fact that I wouldn't get another opportunity to "hunt deer" until the next fall was as much, if not more, a part of the feeling. Reflecting on the past two months of deer hunting while waiting for my ride, I realized my lengthy season had been successful even though a deer wasn't tagged. A variety of experiences helped make it so.

One of the experiences revolved around a white weasel that came by my stand on the second day of the regular firearms hunt. Despite the fact the weasel was wearing his winter coat of white, he stood out in sharp contrast to his surroundings since there wasn't any snow on the ground then.

The streamlined predator thoroughly investigated a brush pile next to me, then started away after finding no prey. A squeak from my lips that imitated the sound a small mammal might make stopped the weasel in his tracks. After staring in bewilderment into the brush pile, he dove back in for another look around.

Then a red squirrel got into the act. It apparently saw the off-colored animal and came to investigate.

The squirrel made a couple of passes at the weasel as it came out of the brush pile for the second time. Oddly enough, the predator dodged the advances of the squirrel rather than attacking. Maybe he was still confused about the source of the squeak. At any rate, I let the weasel continue on its way that time, chuckling to myself as it went.

I have found that deer hunting is more than hours spent in the field with the sole intent of getting a shot at a whitetail or muley. Deer hunting is a total immersion in the outdoors. From my point of view, any experience that makes the hunter feel more like a part of the outdoors has to be considered a success. Seeing deer, shooting deer, can be part of that success, but it doesn't have to be.

Success is the sum total of all the experiences on a deer hunt that make the hunter's days afield worthwhile. The little and big things that make his time in the outdoors richer. Hearing, seeing, and interacting

This white weasel added success to a day of deer hunting.

242

with all forms of wildlife, like the weasel I mentioned, is part of the success of a deer hunt to me.

There are other things, too, like witnessing a beautiful sunrise or being so enchanted with the stillness of the forest you hesitate to interrupt it by moving. Many of the experiences that add to the success of a hunt are difficult to share with others. They can't be brought home like a deer. Even fellow hunters may find it hard to appreciate the singular value of your particular moments in the field.

Experiences that add to the success of a hunt are not always individual things. Good companionship and sharing the good fortune of another member of the party who tagged a deer are also part of it. The afternoon I saw the white weasel, my brother dropped a six-point buck. His success made my day more successful.

If downing a deer were necessary for every hunter to have a successful hunt, the number of those going afield after deer each year would be declining. Instead, their ranks are increasing. Only a small percentage of those who go afield score. The remainder find something attractive about deer hunting other than the kill that brings them back year after year. Most men enjoy a hunt without bagging a deer: success without success.

Success without success is one of the easiest things to accomplish on a deer hunt. No one can tell hunters how to do it; it just happens by being there. Consistently being successful in collecting a whitetail or mule deer, on the other hand, is one of the most difficult aspects of deer hunting. That is why this book and others like it devote most of their content to the know-how involved in getting close enough to deer to shoot them rather than the peripheral joys of deer hunting.

I think such lopsided treatment tends to emphasize the kill rather than the hunt and its sidelights, no matter how unintentional this highlighting is. But the trees, plants, shrubs, insects, birds, reptiles, amphibians, and mammals other than deer are just as much a part of the deer hunter's world as whitetails and muleys.

As I mentioned in previous chapters, killing a deer should be considered a bonus of the hunt. If it is viewed as a necessary part, few will be truly successful.

Seeing that white weasel and sharing in my brother's kill were only a couple of highlights of the year that I didn't get a deer. One extremely successful day during the muzzle-loading season I saw no less than 33 deer. Every last one of them was bald—no antlers. Only antlered bucks were legal during the hunt, but it was nice to look over that many animals. The frequent sightings kept up my hopes of eventually seeing a buck.

I congratulate my brother on his kill. I shared his success.

A comical show put on by a ruffed grouse that day made it a little more successful. All the trees were coated with ice from freezing drizzle. The bird landed in a maple tree near me to pick at buds. It was slipping and sliding as it tried to maintain a grip on the icy branches. From its actions the grouse looked intoxicated.

The more I thought about the days I hunted deer as I waited for my ride on that last day of hunting, the more I realized how successful they had been. I smiled as I remembered an antler I found in December. I was hunting with bow and arrow then. There were three of us, and I was making a drive toward my friends Bill and Kirwin when I spotted an antler in the snow. It had four points. The beam had been shed recently, there was still blood on the base.

I tucked the shed antler in my pocket and when I reached my partners I tried to convince them I got a shot at a buck and my arrow knocked the antler off. I have a hard time keeping a straight face when trying to fool someone. They knew I was pulling their legs.

One-antlered buck Kirwin collected also added success to my otherwise unsuccessful season.

245

Two days later Kirwin arrowed a beautiful buck that had shed one antler. It wasn't the same animal that dropped the antler I found, though. The beam remaining on the deer's head was much more massive than the one I picked up. The deer was killed miles from where we had been before, too.

Kirwin's success and finding that shed antler contributed to my successful year of deer hunting.

My reminiscing was cut short by approaching headlights that I knew would be my partner. "Maybe Bill got one," I thought to myself. But I knew it didn't matter. The collective seasons had been successful even though I didn't get a deer. Bill would feel the same way if he hadn't scored.

Conclusion

Writing about deer hunting is great, but it doesn't get as high a rating from me as actual hunting. Since Michigan's firearms deer season arrived before I completed this book, I took time out to take part. After all, I reasoned, it would be an opportunity to do some last-minute research.

I got a deer, a buck, the day after Thanksgiving. He had three points. Antlerless deer weren't legal in the area I hunted. It took me six days of hunting to connect. I spent better than sixty hours in the field hunting, and the kill took all of five seconds. I'm not complaining; I'm just pointing out that there is a lot more to hunting than killing.

It was 11:30 in the morning when the yearling buck walked past my stand. My vigil began four hours earlier at first light. There was snow on the ground. The evergreen trees surrounded me. It was windy and cold.

There was a noise off to my right. When I looked, my buck was there, 35 to 40 yards away, moving across a small opening at a brisk walking pace. The antlers were easy to see against the backdrop of snow. He was in the scope as soon as I brought the rifle up.

The crosshairs were on his shoulder as he passed through a small opening between two trees. I waited. If I would have shot then, I think my bullet would have hit further back than I wanted because of the deer's speed.

He was in a bigger opening in a fraction of a second. The crosshairs were on the mark, and I squeezed the trigger. My 150-grain soft-point knocked the whitetail off his feet, dead instantly. The bullet hit where the neck joins the body.

An hour later I was relaxing at my post after dressing the deer and taking some photos. I took a bite out of a sandwich from my lunch and saw another deer just beyond where my buck had fallen. Seconds later, a huge eight- or ten-point buck walked quickly through an opening.

It may have been the same buck I saw two days earlier from the same stand. He was running then; so there was no time for a shot. Maybe that buck will be around next year.

I had seen still another buck earlier in the season. This one was in heavy brush. I didn't shoot at that one on the chance he would present a more open shot. He didn't.

The deer were moving more the day I got my buck than they had the entire season. My brother may have helped the situation. He was tracking during most of the morning and may have pushed my buck into me.

While dragging the whitetail I shot to my car, a strange thing happened. At one point a doe came bounding through the hardwoods, bleating as she went. She circled downwind of me and stopped no more than 40 yards away. The deer stood there for some time looking at me and calling. I think she was in estrus (ready to breed) and smelled the buck. Eventually, she left.

The sound the doe made is hard to describe, but I'll bet if a commercial call could be manufactured to imitate it bucks would be attracted by the sound during the rut.

You may be wondering why it took me six days to collect a deer. It wasn't because I didn't scout my area ahead of the season. I did. The stand I picked for opening day looked good, but I didn't see anything there. That's right, not one deer! The weather may have contributed to my failure. It was foggy and drizzly all day.

There was success that day among the Smith party though. Uncle George got a spikehorn first thing in the morning. I spent several hours helping him get it out of the woods.

The third member of our party, my brother Bruce, missed a shot at a buck while still-hunting the second day of the season. Now with two people to move deer for him there is a good chance he will fill his tag before the season is over.

I have learned a lot about deer and deer hunting while writing this book. If you learn something, too, it will have been worth my time in the writing and yours in the reading. I wish I could say everything there is to know about deer and deer hunting is included in these pages, but it's not. There is a lot of information though, enough that I hope this book will be beneficial to a lot of people who, like me, are interested in deer—hunters and nonhunters alike.

There is one last point about hunting deer that I want to make before closing: luck plays as much a part, if not more, in the success of some hunters as skill or knowledge. You can apply every last bit of how-to information in this book and still not get a deer. Yet, another guy who heads into the field deer hunting for the first time in his life and doesn't know a thing about the pursuit can kill a trophy buck.

It is hard to understand, but it happens. Deer are simply not predictable all the time. Nonetheless, for consistent success it pays to be as conscientious and as knowledgeable as possible.

Deer hunting has its share of disappointments, but there are also rewards. Most of the time rewards overshadow disappointments. I know they have for me. The greatest benefit I derive from deer hunting is its contribution to my good health—both physical and mental. I hope deer hunting is at least as rewarding for you.

Bibliography

Brakefield, Tom. *The Sportsman's Complete Book of Trophy and Meat Care*. Harrisburg, Pa., Stackpole Books, 1975.

————. *Hunting Big-Game Trophies: A North American Guide*. New York: E. P. Dutton & Co., 1976.

Brister, Bob. "Rattle 'Em Up, But Safely." *Field & Stream,* vol. 130, no. 8, December 1975, pp. 42–48.

Carmichel, Jim. "Good Gun Care in Foul Weather." *Outdoor Life,* vol. 156, no. 5, pp. 90–94, November 1975.

————. "Sight In Now." *Outdoor Life,* vol. 158, no. 4, October 1976, pp. 94–102.

Cartier, John O. "Guide to Hunting Deer from a Stand." *Outdoor Life,* vol. 156, no. 4, October 1975, pp. 85–92.

Dalrymple, Byron W. *The Complete Book of Deer Hunting*. New York: Winchester Press, 1973.

East, Ben. "The Big Lie." *Outdoor Life,* vol. 149, no. 6, June 1972, pp. 65–67, 100–106.

Elman, Robert (Ed.), *All About Deer Hunting in America*. New York: Winchester Press, 1976.

Fawcett, Joel S. "Try This for Whitetails." *Sports Afield,* vol. 160, no. 3, September 1968, pp. 44–45, 120–121.

Geagan, Bill. "How Indians Hunt Deer." *Field & Stream,* vol. 125, no. 8, December 1970, pp. 36–37, 59–66.

Harbour, Dave. "21 Deer Taking Tips." *Sports Afield,* vol. 170, no. 3, September 1973, pp. 46–50, 139–141.

Helgeland, Glenn. "What the Compound Bow Will Do." *Field & Stream,* vol. 131, no. 6, October 1976, pp. 82–89.

Kal, Paula D. "A Cold Woman Never Got a Whitetail." *The American Rifleman,* vol. 125, no. 1, February 1977, pp. 28–29.

Koller, Lawrence R. *Shots At Whitetails.* New York: Knopf, 1970.

Meryl, Karl and Boue, Ken. *The Deer of Nebraska.* Nebraska Game & Parks Commission Bulletin.

Miller, Peter. "Masters of the Tracker's Art." *Sports Afield,* vol. 172, no. 4, October 1974, pp. 60–63, 166–172.

O'Connor, Jack. "Sighting In Your Rifle." *Outdoor Life,* vol. 148, no. 4, October 1971, pp. 96–100, 104–106.

————. "Where to Place the Shot on Big Game." *Outdoor Life,* vol. 147, no. 1, January 1971, pp. 90–99.

Oertle, V. Lee. "Mule Deer Are Where You Find Them." *Outdoor Life,* Vol. 160, No. 1, July 1977, pp. 76–79, 144.

"Planning a Big Game Hunt." *The American Hunter,* vol. 5, no. 8, August 1977, pp. 69–123.

Richardson, Arthur H. and Petersen, Lyle E. *History and Management of South Dakota Deer.* South Dakota Department of Game, Fish & Parks, Bulletin No. 5, 1974.

Schuyler, Keith. *Bowhunting for Big Game.* Harrisburg, Pa.: Stackpole Books, 1974.

Slade, Glenn. "How to Rattle Up a Buck." *Sports Afield,* vol. 172, no. 5, November 1974, pp. 47, 133–139.

BIBLIOGRAPHY

Stone, Jim. "After Your Deer Is Hit." *Archery World,* vol. 22, no. 5, September 1973, pp. 24–28.

Taylor, Walter Penn. *The Deer of North America.* Harrisburg, Pa.: Stackpole Co., 1956.

Wootters, John. "Of Peeps & Posts." *Field & Stream,* vol. 131, no. 12, April 1977, pp. 142–145.

Index